# THE *Fruit*
## OF THE SPIRIT IS . . .
# *Peace*

# THE *Fruit*
# OF THE SPIRIT IS . . .
# *Peace*

### A small group Bible study

### Lynn Stanley

For the reader's convenience, the author cites verses from the King James *and* the New International Versions of the Bible. The translations appear side-by-side, with the NIV always appearing to the *left* of the KJV.

FOCUS
PUBLISHING
502 Third Street N.W.
Bemidji, MN 56601

# THE *Fruit* OF THE SPIRIT IS ... *Peace*

A small group Bible study

Lynn Stanley

Copyright © 2001 by Focus Publishing
Bemidji, Minnesota 56601
All Rights Reserved

Scripture (KJV) taken from The King James Version and
(NIV) The Holy Bible, International Version ©.
Copyright © 1973, 1978, 1984, by the International Bible Society.
Used by permission of Zondervan Publishing House.

ISBN 1-885904-27-4

Cover Design By Richard Schaefer

Printed in the United States of America

# From the Author

The Holy Spirit of God is not an apparition; He is a real person, who dwells in the heart of all who believe on the Name of Jesus Christ (1 Corinthians 6:19), trust in Him as Savior (Ephesians 1:13), and follow the commandments of God (1 John 3:24). The author would be remiss in offering a study on the fruit of the Holy Spirit without first stressing the need for all who read it to be saved:

> *...I tell you the truth, no one can see the kingdom of God unless he is born again. ...No one can enter the kingdom of God unless he is born of water and the Spirit.*
> **— John 3:3, 5 NIV**

> *...*"*The word is near you; it is in your mouth and in your heart,*"*that is, the word of faith we are proclaiming: That if you confess with your mouth,* "*Jesus is Lord,*"*and believe in your heart that God raised him from the dead, you will be saved. For it is with your heart that you believe and are justified, and it is with your mouth that you confess and are saved.*"
> **— Romans 10:8-10**

> *And you also were included in Christ when you heard the word of truth, the gospel of your salvation. Having believed, you were marked in him with a seal, the promised Holy Spirit.*
> **— Ephesians 1:13**

All who desire to fully experience the supernatural power of God's Holy Spirit, must first confess their sins, being fully repentant, and open to God's intervention in their lives. Second, they must believe that Jesus Christ died for their sins, was buried, rose from the dead, and lives today.

# Introduction

The hustle and bustle of today's culture has not deterred some ladies from canning and freezing their garden bounty for the winter months ahead. The sight of rows and rows of canned fruit and vegetables provides a deep personal satisfaction and peace. There is a sense of successful stewardship of God's provision and our time.

As Christians we need not rely on the fleeting moments of peaceful experiences. God desires that we live within the atmosphere of His constant peace, even when circumstances attempt to rob us of that peace. Lynn Stanley has written this second book in a series of studies on the Fruit of the Spirit to biblically address areas in our lives which can affect our peace. Jesus said…

> ..."Peace I leave with you; my Peace I give you. I do not give to you as the world gives. Do not let your hearts be troubled and do not be afraid." — **John 14:27**

As with each Spiritual fruit, peace grows only when it is nourished by Living Water. None of the Fruits of the Spirit are produced on our own; each is a gift of the Holy Spirit grown out of an abiding faith in the Lord Jesus Christ. If saving faith in Jesus Christ is not accompanied by a desire to make Him Lord of your life, the fruits of God's Spirit will wither on your vine. If the sincere desire of your heart is to grow in the knowledge of Jesus Christ and His Holy Spirit, we are confident that God will use this study to encourage you.

# Contents

**peace 1:** a state of tranquillity or quiet: as **a** : freedom from civil disturbance **b** : a state of security or order within a community provided for by law or custom **2** : freedom from disquieting or oppressive thoughts or emotions; **3** : harmony in personal relations

*Peace I leave with you; my peace I give you. I do not give to you as the world gives. Do not let your hearts be troubled and do not be afraid.* **John 14:27 (NIV)**

# Chapter 1

# The Source
# of True Peace

*Peace I leave with you; my peace I give*
*you. I do not give to you as the world gives.*
*Do not let your hearts be troubled and do*
*not be afraid.*         **John 14:27 (NIV)**

*I am always content with what happens;*
*for I know that what God chooses is better*
*than what I choose.*

**– Epictetus**

I recently heard a poignant story of persecuted Christians in North
Korea. It was reported that Communist soldiers gathered a number of
Christians, lined them up, and placed a picture of Jesus Christ on the floor
near the first man in line. Then one of the soldiers instructed all those in
line to walk past the picture, and spit on it. Anyone who did not do as the
soldier ordered, they said, would be shot to death. The first man to spit on
the picture was a leader in the church. Several men and women followed
his example, before a sixteen-year-old girl stopped, bent to pick up the
picture, and using the hem of her skirt, carefully wiped the spittle from it.
Then, holding the picture against her heart, she looked directly into the
eyes of the soldier with the gun, and calmly said, "I will die for my Jesus."

Nonplussed, the soldier quickly ordered her to leave the room, and
told all those behind her to follow. Barely outside, the startled Christians
heard several shots. They turned to see that the soldiers had opened fire
on all those who had spat upon the picture. They killed them all, reasoning that if they would not be loyal to their God, they would not be loyal to
their government.

Reported to be a true story, that is a dramatic example of the way in which the *peace* of the Holy Spirit is able to prevail in the lives of believers, even under the most extreme circumstances. It parallels the example of Stephen, who despite false accusations against him, spoke up boldly for Jesus Christ. It was the *peace* of the indwelling Holy Spirit that enabled Stephen to stand so calmly in front of his accusers, that they described him as having a "face like the face of an angel." Later, when his persecutors surrounded him, "furiously gnashing their teeth," Stephen was not filled with panic or fear. Instead, he calmly told them that he "saw heaven open and the Son of Man standing at the right hand of God." As they stoned him, Stephen prayed: "Lord Jesus, receive my spirit." Then, Scripture tells us, after asking God to forgive his attackers, he simply *"fell asleep."* (Acts 6:8-7)

Epictetus, (quoted above) was a Stoic philosopher. True Stoics are known for their ability to face any calamity – even death – with perfect calm. Like Epictetus, both Saint Stephen and the young Korean girl lived lives more peaceful than most because they trusted God and they understood His absolute sovereignty in all situations. True peace is a gift of the Spirit to those who believe in God's sovereign ability to control every situation. Peace that remains in the midst of every circumstance is proof of one's confidence that God always knows what is best. Peace that comforts during great tribulation is the result of knowing – absolutely – that God has the power to change any situation at will.

Unfortunately few of us fully trust God at the moment of our salvation. Most of us learn to trust God's sovereignty over a period of time, as He repeatedly demonstrates His power, compassion, and faithfulness during the everyday trials of life. If we are wise, we will acknowledge each of these "tender mercies" as God graciously grants them to us, and we will contemplate His goodness and faithfulness.

As a new Christian, one of my friends began to experience trials he had never faced in the area of finances. For several years, he was tested in his business and in his personal life. Each time, God gave him the gift of faith to trust Him, and repeatedly God rescued my friend from one challenge after another. For example, anticipating a promised promotion at work, my friend bought a new home. By the time he learned that the promotion was going to be given to someone else, his family had already moved in, and his mortgage payment had increased significantly. A few weeks after that, he was involved in a traffic accident in which his car was totaled. Still later, he lost his job altogether when the small, independently-owned company was sold to a large conglomerate.

As my friend waited to find a "good" job, he put his house up for sale and began part-time consulting work to subsidize his family's living expenses. He had been wise and had a savings account, but his savings were almost gone, and as the months stretched into years, his house did not sell, and he still had no permanent job in his field. This continued until my friend was facing financial devastation. He didn't even have enough money in the bank to make his next house payment.

"Over the years," he says now, "...I had spent a lot of time asking God to bail me out. When He did, I was grateful. When He didn't, I learned it was always because He had something to teach me. I accepted God's will regarding my finances because whatever He allowed, I always came out better for it. By the time the 'big bomb' was dropped and I thought I'd lose the house," he says, "...I was so accustomed to dodging missiles that I hardly noticed. My confidence had grown so much from the small things, that I didn't hesitate to trust God for the 'big thing'. I simply resigned myself to the fact that 'my' house wasn't really mine at all. Everything I have is a gift from God and if He wills to take it from me, He will give me the strength and ability to start over.

Fortunately, my friend didn't lose his home. The house finally sold and a few days after that, he had a good job in his field, and it paid him well. In addition to the material blessings he received, he acquired a gift of peace that abides in him still.

Given man's sinful nature, it is doubtful that any human being is born with an innate ability to trust God under all circumstances. At some point, each must *make a choice to believe God's promises* and *apply God's Truth to his life.* If one truly seeks peace, one must (as Epictetus did) *choose to want for himself only what God wants for him.*

| | |
|---|---|
| ***Whatever you have learned or received or heard from me, or seen in me—put it into practice. And the God of peace will be with you.*** <br> **Philippians 4:9(NIV)** | ***Those things, which ye have both learned, and received, and heard, and seen in me, do: and the God of peace shall be with you.* (KJV)** |

The first step toward achieving a peaceful life is to know – absolutely – that the One True God of Heaven is the only source of true and lasting contentment. Only those who know God's Word and obey it will experience the genuine supernatural peace that comes from God alone.

*I have told you these things, so that in me you may have peace. In this world you will have trouble. But take heart! I have overcome the world.* **John 16:33 (NIV)**

*These things I have spoken unto you, that in me ye might have peace. In the world ye shall have tribulation: but be of good cheer; I have overcome the world." (KJV)*

Health professionals claim that on average, only 5% of the things most people worry about actually happen. That means that 95% of the time spent worrying could be more effectively spent on something else. Matthew 7 tells believers not to worry about anything. We worship *Jehovah-jireh*- "the God who provides" (Genesis 22:8). Those who worship the One True God and follow the Lord Jesus Christ need never worry about the basic necessities of life: what they will eat, drink, or wear. *Worry,* Jesus Himself implies, only steals precious hours from our lives (Matthew 7: 25-27) – time much better spent in worship and prayer.

For three years, Nancy had been in charge of the devotional time for her neighborhood Bible study. A diligent student of the Scriptures, she came prepared each week to help the women focus their thoughts on Jesus before the group study time began. One day, immediately following an inspirational few minutes in which Nancy spoke of the benefits of trusting God, she surprised everyone by breaking down in tears. She wasn't just crying, she was *sobbing.*

"I just couldn't stop," she said. "Suddenly I was overwhelmed, feeling that I was nothing but a hypocrite! There I was, telling others to trust God when I didn't trust Him myself.

"That morning before I went to Bible study I had been praying about our finances." She paused momentarily and then confessed: "Well, actually I had been *worrying* about our finances. Our house payment was due the next day, and we were seventy-five dollars short of making the payment. Jeff had been out of work for five months, and there was just no money.

"I wasn't crying because we didn't have the money; I was crying because I felt so spiritually inadequate. I was thinking that if I really trusted God, I would have peace – with or without that money in the bank.

"We were a very close group and everyone in the Bible study knew that Jeff was out of work. They had been praying for us ever since he lost his job. Because I seldom miss a day reading Scripture, I am almost always spiritually strong and positive about things. But for some reason, that day I just lost it. I was crying so hard that one of the other women led me out of the room so we could talk privately.

"After I had my cry, we discussed the situation and the two of us prayed together. It was one of those miraculous times when God—in His mercy—teaches us how to live. I came away from that prayer time feeling much better because God helped me to see that I wasn't as much *worried* as I was *concerned* – and there is a big difference!

"I began to see myself as *God* was seeing me: I had done pretty well since Jeff lost his job—resting in God's sovereignty, and trusting Him to provide. Up until that morning, I really hadn't worried the whole time. I'm not saying I didn't *think* about our situation, but I really wasn't worried about it. Whenever I caught myself thinking about the fact that we had no income, I just recited that simple verse of Scripture: *God will provide.* That truth is always soothing to me because I believe it. Since I've been a Christian, God *has* provided in every situation. But for some reason, I didn't think about Scripture that morning. All I thought about was: *It's the fourth of the month, our payment is due tomorrow, and we don't have enough money!*

"Instead of *fixing my eyes on Jesus* [Hebrews 12:1-2], my eyes were fixed on myself and my circumstance. Before I realized it, my *concern* had turned to *worry,* and worry is a sin.

"During that prayer time with my friend, it dawned on me that any rational human being would be concerned about a problem like mine. Concern is thinking about something that matters in your life, and not being able to pay for the roof over your head certainly qualifies as something that matters! But worry is the result of anxiety over the things that concern us. When the Lord showed me that difference, I was able to consider my feelings objectively. Suddenly I realized that concern over problems is normal, but worry is always a sin. If I believe that God knows what I need—and I *do* believe that—I must choose to trust Him.

"I did so and immediately, I felt better. I came away from that short time of prayer a different person, more confident than ever in God, and knowing that whatever happens, He is always in control and He will never forsake us.

"In one of His awesome ways, God affirmed my confidence just a few hours later. When I got home there was a check in our mail box for $125.00 – *more* than we needed! A few months before, I had recommended a contractor to some friends who were remodeling their home. They hired him and as a thank you, he sent us a 'finder's fee'!"

By studying Scripture, we gain knowledge of God as He reveals His attributes to us: His concern for us, His compassion and mercy, His boundless love, His absolute sovereignty, His infinite wisdom, His incredible grace—and His desire and promise to provide all that we need to live lives free from worry:

*And my God will meet all your needs according to his glorious riches in Christ Jesus.*
**Philippians 4:19 (NIV)**

*But my God shall supply all your need according to his riches in glory by Christ Jesus.* **(KJV)**

Scripture tells us what God does – and will do – for us to insure that we may have peace in our lives. It also tells us what *we* must do: how we must live, and in whom we must place our trust and hope if we are to experience true contentment. The problem is not that we cannot know how to attain peace, because God's Word *tells* us exactly what we must do. The problem is that many who read God's truth do not apply it to their lives.

## A lamp unto my path...

We must be cautious not to confuse knowledge and wisdom: knowledge helps one make a *living*, but wisdom helps one make a *life*. *Wisdom is the application of knowledge.* Wisdom happens when we choose to claim victory over our circumstances because of God's specific promises.

For example, when payday is a week away and the cupboard is nearly bare, we can pray Matthew 6:11: "Give us today our daily bread." Such a prayer with its implied promise belongs to those who worship *Jehovah-Jireh,* the God who provides.

Scripture tells us that fear of the Lord is the beginning of knowledge (Proverbs 1:7) *and* the beginning of wisdom (Proverbs 9:10). The word "fear" implies *reverential awe.* In other words, those who fear the Lord will respectfully consider God's existence and seriously ponder the reality of His active involvement in their lives—in *all* circumstances.

Wisdom implies that we make a conscious choice to respond in a specific way because of the knowledge we possess. For example, if I were to learn that my husband and I were going to lose our life's savings, I could choose to doubt God, or I could choose to trust Him because He has promised to provide all that we need. Either way, I make a conscious choice to believe God's Word, or not.

| | |
|---|---|
| *...I do not concern myself with great matters or things too wonderful for me. But I have stilled and quieted my soul;...* | *...neither do I exercise myself in great matters, or in things too high for me. Surely I have behaved and quieted myself,...* **(KJV)** |

**Psalm 131:1B-2A (NIV)**

*Knowledge* of God's Word is the shield that protects us from the fiery arrows of doubt. But as with any shield, God's Word will only protect us if we stand behind it. Scripture says, *"wisdom is better than weapons of war"* (Ecclesiastes 9:18). It isn't enough just to possess knowledge; we must *use* it wisely and to our benefit. Doubt in God's ability to provide for us comes from the enemy who seeks to destroy our faith. Doubt is a weapon of spiritual war.

Romans 8:32 declares that God *"did not spare his own Son, but gave him up for us all—how will he not also, along with him, graciously give us all things?"* Wisdom tells me that if God loved me enough to send Jesus to die for me, He will certainly give me all that I need to live. Knowledge tells me that my husband and I *could* be in big trouble if we lost our life's savings, but wisdom tells me that we will survive because I know I can trust God in any circumstance.

## "...by my Spirit," says the Lord

God *knows* how difficult it is to live the Christian life – to imitate Christ in faith and obedience – and He knows that none of us can do it in our own strength:

*...Not by might nor by power, but by my Spirit," says the Lord Almighty.* **Zechariah 4:6 (NIV)**

*...Not by might, nor by power, but by my spirit, saith the Lord of hosts.* **(KJV)**

Even the disciples, blessed to experience the person of Jesus Christ in the flesh, needed more than Christ's example to live God's way:

*After his suffering, he showed himself to these men and gave many convincing proofs that he was alive. He appeared to them over a period of forty days and spoke about the kingdom of God. On one occasion, while he was eating with them, he gave them this command: "Do not leave Jerusalem, but wait for the gift my Father promised, which you have heard me speak about. For John baptized with water, but in a few days you will be baptized with the Holy Spirit." So when they met together, they asked him, "Lord, are you at this time going to restore the Kingdom to Israel?" He said to them, "It is not for you to know the times or dates the Father has set by his own authority. But you will receive power when the Holy Spirit comes on you; and you will be my witnesses in Jerusalem, and in all Judea and Samaria, and to the ends of the earth." (Acts 1:3-8)*

*To whom also he showed himself alive after his passion by many infallible proofs, being seen of them forty days, and speaking of the things pertaining to the kingdom of God: And, being assembled together with them, commanded them that they should not depart from Jerusalem, but wait for the promise of the Father, which, saith he, ye have heard of me. For John truly baptized with water; but ye shall be baptized with the Holy Ghost not many days hence. When they therefore were come together, they asked of him, saying, Lord wilt thou at this time restore again the kingdom to Israel? And he said unto them, It is not for you to know the times or the seasons, which the Father hath put in his own power. But ye shall receive power, after that the Holy Ghost is come upon you: and ye shall be witnesses unto me both in Jerusalem, and in all Judea, and in Samaria, and unto the uttermost part of the earth.*

Once we admit that we cannot live life effectively on our own, we are free to tap into the supernatural power of God, promised to all who trust Jesus Christ as Savior:

| | |
|---|---|
| ***Because you are sons, God sent the Spirit of his Son into our hearts, the Spirit who calls out, "Abba, Father."*** **Galatians 4:6 (NIV)** | ***And because ye are sons, God hath sent forth the Spirit of his Son into your hearts, crying, Abba, Father.*** **(KJV)** |

"Abba" is a term of endearment. It is the English equivalent of "Daddy." Consider what that means: The Almighty God of Heaven promises each individual believer an intimate, loving, relationship with Himself, through His indwelling Holy Spirit. Imagine yourself, sitting in the lap of God with the Heavenly Father's arms around you. His ear is bent intently toward you – *His child* – because He wants to hear the most intimate desires of your heart. What are they? Do you want money? A mate? A better marriage? A child? A child who obeys? A bigger home? A newer car? A promotion? What would make you content? What would give you peace?

Many of us find that no matter how much God gives us, we're never quite "there." We seldom experience true contentment because we always want something else, something more, or something different. Socrates said: "He who is not contented with what he has, would not be *contented with what he would like to have."*

Sadly, in our pursuit of *things* we not only neglect God, we often fail to acknowledge or thank Him for all He graciously provides. For example, the "take-it-for-granted-blessings" of every-day life: food, shelter, clothing, health, and the very breath that enables us to live each day. While we are consumed with visions of how much better our lives would be *if only...,* we seldom ponder what life would be like if God chose to withhold even *one* of those take-it-for-granted-blessings from us: How do you think you would feel if you arrived home one afternoon and saw nothing but ashes where your house used to stand? How long would you live if God chose to withhold your food and water? How would you survive in today's world with only a dollar in your wallet? What if you learned that you have a terminal illness? Most of us run to the Heavenly Father when our survival—or even our comfort level—is threatened. Whenever adversity comes, we become passionate in prayer, imploring God to help us. But few of us are equally impassioned about thanking Him for what we already have. I challenge you to let your last thoughts at night be praise and gratitude to God for everything that *could* have happened that day, and didn't.

In God's economy, *He* is all we need: More of *Him* is what He wants us to desire: more of His character, more of His Word, more of His Law, more of His love and mercy. To live for God, to work for Him, to give Him our time, our talent and our treasure, is to honor Him for all that He gives us.

Peace *can* be in the heart of every believer, but only when each understands that genuine contentment only comes when our hearts are in accord with God's—when we want what *He* wants for us.

## Life Application: Chapter One

### Day One:
Read Psalm 62:1-2 and Acts 10:34-36. From where does true peace come?

Romans 8:6 says, *"the mind controlled by the Spirit is life and peace."* Read the following verses and record the ways in which one can bring his/her mind under the control of the Holy spirit.

Joshua 1:8

2 Corinthians 10:4-5

Philippians 4:8

### Day Two:
Read the following verses and record what each says about the Holy Spirit:

(Example) John 14:26 tells us *He teaches*

John 16:12-15

Romans 15:30-33

Ephesians 4:30

In the space below, record a specific example of a time when you know the Holy Spirit's supernatural power was manifest in your life. For example, did God allow you to accomplish something that you had thought impossible? Perhaps He allowed you to speak the truth boldly

when you thought yourself unable to do so?

How did you feel, the first time you realized that the supernatural power of God was available to you?

**Day Three:**

Read Psalm 78:17-22. How does God feel about those who fail to trust in Him?

In spite of the Israelite's failure to trust Him, what did God do for His people? Psalm 78:23-25

Why do you think God continues to bless His children, in spite of their grumbling?

What does Lamentations 3:37-40 say about adversity *and* blessing?

What do these verses suggest about one possible *reason* for adversity?

In your quiet time, ask God to show you (specifically) the areas in which you must trust Him more. In the space below, list those areas. For example, if you often worry about money, you are not trusting God to provide for you; write *"finances."*

- 
- 
- 

**Day Four:**
Read Matthew 6:31-34. In the space below, record Jesus' command in V. 31.

What label does Jesus give to those who worry about the necessities of life? V. 32

According to V. 33, what are the only two things a child of God should seek after?

What is the end-result for those who seek God's kingdom and His righteousness? V.33

What do you think Jesus means when He says, *"all these things"*?

## Day Five:

Go through Chapter One and *re-read the Scriptures* in bold print within the text. In the space below, summarize what God has revealed to you through your study:

# Chapter 2

# At Peace With God

*"Submit to God and be at peace with him;*
*in this way prosperity will come to you."*
**Job 22:21**

*Peace is the certain portion of the child*
*of God who is in the will of God.*
**– Amy Carmichael**

Abiding peace is the result of a conscious and reverent respect for the sovereignty and will of God. Scripture commands us to *submit* to God…to surrender *all* to Him: every desire, every sin, every worry, every relationship, and every material possession. True submission means that we agree to yield totally to the will of God, even when His will for us is not what we will for ourselves. Those who submit to God can do so because they understand His sovereignty and His perfect love for His children.

*Because God is sovereign* (in control of all things), whatever is happening to us is being *allowed* by Him to happen. Genuine peace results from one's choice to accept whatever God allows because we know that in the end, God wills that all things work together for the good of those who love Him (Romans 8:28).

Control of the will is the very essence of spiritual warfare. At the root of every conflict is the fight between our own will and God's will *for* us. Though situations and temptations vary, every problem, every circumstance, every temptation boils down to one issue: To whom do we give the control of our will? Until the believer has settled that issue in his mind, the human heart will remain conflicted and restless. For example, when we suffer (or fear that we may have to suffer) we are likely filled with anxiety instead of tranquility. Such feelings are not unusual for those who have no faith, but for those blessed with the promises of God, such feelings are more than foolish, they are evidence of doubt in God's ability to keep His promises. You may think, *if God gives me the flu, I can live with that, but He better not give me cancer.* Such thinking indicates lack of faith in God's goodness in what He allows for His glory.

*Praise the Lord, O my soul; all my inmost being, praise his holy name. Praise the Lord, O my soul, and forget not all his benefits – who forgives all your sins and heals all your diseases.* **Psalm 103:1-3 (NIV)**

*Bless the Lord, O my soul: and all that is within me, bless his holy name. Bless the Lord, O my soul, and forget not all his benefits: Who forgiveth all thine iniquities; who healeth all thy diseases; (KJV)*

*He heals the brokenhearted and binds up their wounds.*
**Psalm 147:3 (NIV)**

*He healeth the broken in heart, and bindeth up their wounds.* **(KJV)**

Sometimes conflict arises because we "make deals" with God. We may submit by accepting a lousy relationship, but we refuse to believe that God *really* expects us to forgive as He forgives us, or to love the unlovable as He does. He is, after all, *God. He* has (we tell ourselves) what we do *not*— supernatural power. To think that God cannot heal hearts and feelings is to deny His perfect love. To think that *we* cannot forgive, is to deny the transforming and supernatural power of the Holy Spirit that is promised to every true believer. When we accept Christ as Savior *and make Him Lord of our lives,* God puts a new heart in us and gives us the mind of Christ with which to reason His will for us.

*I will give you a new heart and put a new spirit in you; I will remove from you your heart of stone and give you a heart of flesh.*
**Ezekiel 36:26 (NIV)**

*A new heart also will I give you, and a new spirit will I put within you: and I will take away the stony heart out of your flesh, and I will give you an heart of flesh. (KJV)*

*"For who has known the mind of the Lord that he may instruct him?" But we have the mind of Christ.* **1 Corinthians 2:16 (NIV)**

*For who hath known the mind of the Lord, that he may instruct him? But we have the mind of Christ.* **(KJV)**

Submission to God's will is about the issue of *Lordship.* Those who say they believe in the power of the resurrected Christ must actively demonstrate that belief by giving Him complete control of their lives. That means taking full advantage of every opportunity to demonstrate overtly to others that *God can be trusted.* In spite of one's circumstances, there is no limit to God's power in the life of the believer. When we say, "I cannot" we really mean, "I *will* not:" I *will* not to believe that I can do all things through Christ, who strengthens me.... I *could* choose to submit to God's will for me in this situation but instead, I will *not* to trust Him for its outcome.

Few of us view suffering as a positive thing, but Scripture tells us suffering is even more than that. Paul says it has been *granted* to us on behalf of Christ not only to believe on Him, but also to suffer for Him (Philippians 1:29). The word *granted* means "to be given as a precious gift." If we would view suffering from Paul's perspective, we would be in a position to benefit from it. Submission to the will of God would be easy if one could see past the temporal discomfort of pain and view it as a seed sown for the purpose of spiritual growth.

The question now becomes: *How do I do that? How do I rest in God's will? How do I change my perspective in order to see every circumstance as an opportunity for blessing?* Like the Gospel message itself, the answer is so simple that few believe it: *It is a matter of faith.*

Few take time to contemplate seriously the issue, but submission is the mainstay of all spiritual disciplines. Without a submissive spirit, one does not give the Holy Spirit the freedom to do His work in one's life. To resist the will of God is to interfere with His plan for your life, and to stifle any opportunity to grow spiritually through adversity. Instead of anxiously asking *"Why me, God?"* we can choose to rest in God's will and ask Him to teach us through our pain.

*Consider it pure joy, my brothers, whenever you face trials of many kinds, because you know that the testing of your faith develops perseverance. Perseverance must finish its work so that you may be mature and complete, not lacking anything.* **James 1:2-4 (NIV)**

*My brethren, count it all joy when ye fall into divers temptations; Knowing this, that the trying of your faith worketh patience. But let patience have her perfect work, that ye may be perfect and entire, wanting nothing.* **(KJV)**

Linda sat on the couch, twisting a damp tissue and nervously wrapping it around her finger. She had not slept all night, and it showed. Her eyes were red and swollen, her cheeks raw from rubbing salty tears from her skin. The night before, her fiancé had told her that he did not want to go through with the wedding.

"I just can't believe it," she said. "Why *now?* We've been together for almost five years! I have my *dress!*" There wasn't a specific reason; he said he had just "changed his mind."

As I struggled to find a way to comfort her, several thoughts went through my mind. I was a lay counselor, and my church had assigned Linda to me. She claimed to be a believer, but apart from the fact that she attended church (and sometimes even Bible study), there was little evidence of that in her life. I knew that she frequently spent the night with her fiancé and she did not see a problem with that. As a counselor, I was growing frustrated because in spite of my efforts to change her thinking, Linda had not been convicted about the sin of having sex outside of marriage. In fact, a few days before she called me, I had been thinking about the countless hours I had invested in her without seeing any change in her behavior. I had made a decision to stop counseling her as long as she continued in her sin, but before I could tell her that, she called me with the news that the relationship was over. Now, I was sitting across from her, listening to her sad story and praying that God would give me the wisdom to know what to say. Linda was almost thirty-four years old and she had devoted five years of her life to this guy.... How could I possibly say anything that would help her recover from her loss?

Finally I asked her a simple question: "Linda, do you believe that God is in control of this situation?"

After hesitating, she said, "I *guess* so...."

"Well, don't *guess*," I said. "Based on everything that you know about the God of the Bible, is God in charge or isn't He?"

"He's in charge," she finally admitted, "...but that doesn't mean I understand! Ben won't even *talk* about staying together. He said he's absolutely made up his mind and he doesn't even want to discuss it! Can you *imagine* that? After *five years?* I told him I know I'm not perfect, but I certainly don't deserve *this!*"

"Why?" I asked.

"Why what?"

"Why don't you deserve this?"

From the look on her face I thought I must have been growing another head, right before her eyes. She was staring at me the same way small children stare at movie screens filled with creatures from outer space. Without warning we were in a stare-down, neither of us speaking for what seemed like eternity. All I could do was hold her gaze and pray that God would help me.

Finally she said, "Okay. I get what you mean...."

Now, that surprised me because *I* wasn't exactly sure what I meant! But when one trusts the Holy Spirit to intervene, He does, and before I could respond, Linda continued: "You think that because we were having sex, God punished me by allowing this to happen."

"No," I answered truthfully, "...I don't think that at all. What I think is that if you will allow Him to, God will use this situation to help you grow closer to Him. There is nothing you can do to change this. Ben has made up his mind; he's leaving you. But God will *never* leave you. Long after everyone you love is gone, He will still be there."

Her thoughtful expression indicated that she was considering my words.

"You have to make some choices," I continued. "For one thing, are you going to let this ruin your life? Are you going to listen to the lies of the enemy, who wants to use this situation to destroy you? Or are you going to ask God to teach you through it?"

After a moment she answered with conviction. "I want to learn through it. I know I did things wrong. After I began meeting with you, I started feeling guilty about sleeping with him. I knew it wasn't right. But I was afraid I'd lose him."

I didn't need to point out that she had lost him anyway.

The end result of Linda's experience was that she chose to submit to God's will. Further, she determined—-*by her own will*—to accept her circumstances *willingly;* to receive her suffering as a precious gift *granted to her* from God. She made a verbal commitment to trust God, and she resolved to spend more time in prayer in order to grow closer to Him. In addition to the fact that Linda now feels very strongly about sexual purity, she also realized that she had been living a lie. She recently said, "If I hadn't gone through the breakup with Ben, I never would have sought

God in the way I am seeking Him now. Ben was everything to me that God should have been. I recommitted my life to Christ, and now *He* is the most important 'man' in my life."

I don't want the reader to think that Linda was simply able to turn her emotions off like running water, because that was most certainly not the case. For months following the breakup she was sad and lonely, but eventually she was able to live with her loss. Because Linda *chose* to let go—to surrender her situation completely to the One who loves her most—the power available to her through God's Spirit enabled her to have peace in spite of what was, to her, a dreadful and life-altering circumstance.

When we face trials of any kind, we have choices: We accept the will of God, or we do not. We submit to God, or we fight against Him. We can view difficult circumstances as an opportunity to grow spiritually as we observe God's power, creativity, and faithfulness, or we can refuse those gifts of God and miss His blessings.

Those who lack peace in their lives are holding *on* to their lives. Paul said, *"I have been crucified with Christ; I no longer live, but Christ lives in me"* (Galatians 2:20). To be *crucified with Christ* is to die to self. One who is truly "crucified with Christ" is (relationally speaking) *one with God*—-sharing in His sufferings, filled with His Holy Spirit, and longing to live a sanctified life. To be "crucified" is to be *dead to self.* To surrender *all* to God means that when we claim the Name of Jesus, we also claim the power of His Holy Spirit to sustain us when things get rough. Total surrender and submission to the will of God means that Jesus is not just the Savior of our souls, He is the Lord and Master of our lives *always.* For what good is faith if it is not strong enough to sustain us through adversity?

God is the Designer of all physical matter, wisdom and intelligence. He created the inmost being of every living creature and knit each together in the womb (Psalm 139:13). We are God's "workmanship" (Ephesians 2:10). Because God created you and me, there is nothing He does not know about us. There is no thought or motive, no desire or fear, no sadness or joy that occurs out of view of His watchful eye. God is aware of our past, He is observing each of us in the present, and He knows and sees our future. Our Heavenly Father is always near, always watchful, always protective, and always compassionate. And He is *always desirous of what is best* for His children.

Certain things are true of those who have accepted Jesus Christ as Savior, and made Him the Lord of their lives: We are children of God and part of His family. As such, we are joint heirs with Christ, sharing His inheritance (Romans 8:16-17). We are chosen by God Himself and *appointed by Christ to bear His fruit* (John 15:16). We are "holy and dearly loved" (Colossians 3:12). As children of the Living God, we "have been blessed with every spiritual blessing," and we are "recipients of His *lavish* grace" (Ephesians 1:3, 7-8).

Truly, the gifts of God to all who believe in Jesus Christ are too wonderful to imagine, too extravagant to comprehend. But most significant is the fact Jesus died for us while we were still sinners. As a result of that greatest of all sacrifices—that "indescribable gift"—we have been forgiven of our sins, and resurrection power is available to all believers through the Spirit of the *Living* God. Knowing all that, how is it even *possible* that we sometimes think God will withhold a smaller blessing from us?

| | |
|---|---|
| *He who did not spare his own Son, but gave him up for us all –how will he not also, along with him, graciously give us all things?* <br> **Romans 8:32 (NIV)** | *He that spared not his own Son, but delivered him up for us all, how shall he not with him also freely give us all things?* **(KJV)** |

## His ways are not our ways...

It would be easy to submit to God if we knew ahead of time that everything would turn out the way we want. But surrender is not easy when we fear the unknown. Anxiety over what *could* happen can cause us to become possessive of our problem or sin; we may hold on to it tightly because we fear that if we give it over to God there may be a consequence that we are not willing to accept. For example: *If I take on that responsibility, I might fail.* Or, *if I don't lie for my boss, he might fire me.* So instead of focusing on God's unlimited power to intervene and bless our obedience, we are focused on the situation—and only from our limited human perspective.

Total surrender is an admission that we cannot do it alone: we cannot resist the sin, we cannot survive the illness, we cannot overcome the adversity. In other words, *we cannot succeed at anything without God*. The peace that surpasses all understanding is a fruit of the Holy Spirit grown out of unconditional faith in God *regardless of how things seem*. It means we have a head *and* heart understanding of our total dependence upon Him for everything. True faith says that *with God all things are possible* (Matthew 19:26) and *that* is why it is possible to surrender every situation fully to Him.

When we petition the Lord for the desires of our hearts, we usually neglect to consider His creativity. Instead of relaxing and letting God be God, we set our minds on where we want to go and how we think we are going to get there. With the best of intentions, we study the Map of Success with our eyes glued to the big red curvy lines: the Super Highways. In our haste to get where we want to go in the most expedient way, we forget that God has created myriads of "Blue Highways," too…the smaller, less traveled and more scenic routes that make life's journey interesting.

My husband's profession has required that we move often. Since we married almost thirty-five years ago, we have lived in ten states (several of those more than once) and Puerto Rico, and in too many cities to name. I decided early on that our way of life would require me to adapt quickly to new surroundings. In order to speed up the process, I often took  "adventure days." When Fred left town for work, I would take out a map, pick a town near my new city, and drive there to explore for a day or two. I always avoided the Interstate, taking the back roads because the "adventure" came from not knowing what I would find along the way. The result was almost always the same: serenity, beautiful landscapes, and quaint old towns with Mom-and-Pop restaurants and unique little shops that most people missed because they took the *easy* way; they took the Interstate like everyone else!

Every day is like an "adventure day" when we travel through life with God because He is so incredibly creative. Sometimes we are foolish enough to assume that He will always act on our behalf as any mortal would. What we eventually learn, is that when we walk with God He does not always lead us down the easiest, most efficient road. He takes us down the Blue Highways, where there is much more to observe. It is sometimes inconvenient and less comfortable to travel that way, but once we reach our destination we see clearly that the journey was more productive. If we lack peace because we have not received the thing we want, we must remember that God always knows where our journey will end. And even before we begin, He knows the best and most incredible way to get us there.

*"For my thoughts are not your thoughts, neither are your ways my ways," declares the Lord. "As the heavens are higher than the earth, so are my ways higher than your ways and my thoughts than your thoughts".*    **Isaiah 55:8-9 (NIV)**

*For my thoughts are not your thoughts, neither are your ways my ways, saith the Lord. For as the heavens are higher than the earth, so are my ways higher than your ways, and my thoughts than your thoughts.*            **(KJV)**

*I form the light and create darkness, I bring prosperity and create disaster; I, the Lord, do all these things.*        **Isaiah 45:7 (NIV)**

*I form the light, and create darkness: I make peace, and create evil: I the Lord do all these things.*

            **(KJV)**

## Life Application:

### Day One:

Read Matthew 26:39 and 42. What biblical principle does Jesus demonstrate to us in these verses?

In what way did Jesus learn submission? Hebrews 5:8

In your reading this week, what is the most significant thing you learned about the issue of submission?

List any situations or behaviors that you have not submitted to God. Please give this *prayerful* consideration before you answer. Consider every area of your life: finances, relationships, goals, spiritual life, social habits, etc. *This is your private journal; you will not be asked to share this information with anyone unless you want to in order to benefit someone else.*

Why do you think you have refused to surrender this situation or behavior?

## Day Two:

Read Isaiah 45:7 and Jeremiah 32:27 and record what each says, using your own words.

Read the following verses and record the reasons why peace with God is possible even in the midst of difficult circumstances:

Proverbs 2:7

Psalm 9:9-10

Romans 8:18

1 Peter 4:16

James 1:2-4

## Day Three

Who controls the will of those who do not submit to God? Ephesians 2:1-2

How does Romans 8:6 describe the mind that is controlled by the Holy Spirit?

What does Philippians 4:13 say about our ability to submit to God?

Read 1 Corinthians 10:13. What does it say about temptation?


Scripture commands us to *submit to God* (Job 22:21). Given that command, how do you define those who *do not* submit to God?


Do you believe that failure to submit to God is a sin?
Yes_____ No_____

What does 1 Corinthians 10:13 say about the believer's ability to resist the temptation to sin?




With specific reference to 1 Corinthians 10:13, when is it acceptable for a believer to ignore God's command to submit?


## Day Four
Submission is impossible without trust in the one to whom we are called to submit. List some of the reasons why it is possible to trust God.

Deuteronomy 7:9


Isaiah 26:4


Proverbs 15:3

Psalm 18:30

Psalm 103:11

**Day Five**
What has the Holy Spirit revealed to you about the issue of submission that you did not know before?

*Wisdom is the application of knowledge.* In reference to your response to the question on Day One, "List any situations or behaviors that you have not submitted to God," how will you apply this new knowledge in the area of submission to God?

*Chapter 3*

# Your Heart's Desire

*...I was filled with delight day after day, rejoicing always in his presence, rejoicing in his whole world and delighting in mankind.* **Proverbs 8:30 (NIV)**

Shortly after his throne was established in Israel, King Solomon went to Gibeon, where he offered "a thousand burnt offerings" to the Lord. There the Lord appeared to Solomon in a dream and said, *"Ask for whatever you want me to give you."* Instead of asking for gold or palaces or horses with chariots, Solomon asked for *wisdom.* Specifically, he petitioned God for a discerning heart to govern His people and the ability to distinguish right from wrong.

Solomon's request so delighted the Lord that He not only promised the king long life, He promised him what he did not ask for: *"both riches and honor—so that in your lifetime you will have no equal among kings"* (1 Kings 3: 4-15).

Solomon knew how to delight the Lord. He was a man who "walked in God's ways." Like his father, King David, Solomon kept God's decrees and commands, His laws and requirements (2 Kings 2:3). Because God's Truth was in Solomon's *head,* God's desires were in his *heart.* Solomon knew and believed God's covenant promises because throughout his lifetime, he had observed God's faithfulness to Israel. For that reason, Solomon was not compelled to request what he already knew: God would provide for those who do His will. God will provide everything His people need to sustain a quality of life that is pleasing to Him – and not laden down with things that may distract us from Him.

God blessed Solomon with "riches and honor" not just because Solomon obeyed Him, but because the king had a godly attitude toward material things. Solomon was at peace with God; he was content to bask in the simple blessings that God freely gives to all of His creation, every day: His presence, His world, and all that He created. Or, to borrow a thought from a very wise preacher, one could say that God gave Solomon the desires of his heart because God *was* the desire of his heart.

*...and observe what the Lord your God requires: walk in his ways, and keep his decrees and commands, his laws and requirements, as written in the law of Moses, so that you may prosper in all you do and wherever you go.*

**I Kings 2:3 (NIV)**

*...and keep the charge of the Lord thy God, to walk in his ways, to keep his statutes, and his commandments, and his judgements, and his testimonies, as it is written in the law of Moses, that thouest may prosper in all that thou doest and withersoever thou turnest thyself.* **(KJV)**

It is interesting to note that later in Solomon's life—after he had accumulated more riches and material possessions than probably anyone living on earth—the wisdom God gave him enabled Solomon to understand the absolute futility of a life spent in the pursuit of things. In the first chapter of Ecclesiastes, Solomon refers to all of life as *meaningless* (NIV). Translated, the word means "breath" or "vapor." Solomon is saying that unless one is rightly related to God, nothing in life has any real value. In other words, what possible value can "things" have if the one who possesses them is doomed for eternity?

In wisdom Solomon did more than simply acknowledge God's existence. He seriously contemplated the awesome reality of God's literal presence in his life. He meditated upon the incredible majesty of God's creation and pondered the implications of His grace and mercy. Surely King Solomon's worshipful devotion must have delighted the Lord!

## Seek Ye first...

I once edited a book on biblical finance. The author, Dr. Wilson Humber, is President of a successful investment and estate consulting firm and specializes in helping people prepare for retirement. Dr. Humber asserts that only four out of every one hundred Americans are financially independent at the age of sixty-five. He claims that most of us fail to attain financial security because our lives are not conformed to the biblical standard to *seek God first* (Matthew 6:33). Most of us are poor money managers because we are not content with having what we *need;* we are consumed with trying to get what we *want.*

In our culture it is not uncommon for people to comment on each other's clothes, the model of car they drive, or the type of house they live in. It can be a real challenge to remain content in an atmosphere where comparisons are constantly being made. If we have a decent looking car that starts each time we turn the ignition on, we will likely go for weeks and not even think about it. But when the next-door neighbor gets a new 4 X 4, we may start to think that we'd like one too. If we yield to the pressure of coveting what everyone else has, we allow Satan to steal our enjoyment of that which God has so generously provided.

*Since, then, you have been raised with Christ, set your hearts on things above, where Christ is seated at the right hand of God. Set your minds on things above, not on earthly things.*
**Colossians 3:1-2 (NIV)**

*If ye then be risen with Christ, seek those things which are above, where Christ sitteth on the right hand of God. Set your affection on things above, not on things on the earth.* **(KJV)**

Often the most profound changes in one who is "born again" comes by way of a change in the things he *desires.* For some the change comes quickly and there is an immediate turning away from sin. For others the change is slow as the believer continues to ask God to free him of a habit, lifestyle, or relationship that hinders him spiritually. But for most people, a change in the desires of the heart is neither rapid nor slow, but somewhere in between: As the believer grows in his knowledge of God he begins to see and appreciate God's holiness. Subsequently an appreciation for God's holiness inspires reverence for Him. Ultimately, it is genuine love and reverence for God that convicts the believer of sin and leads him to aspire toward holiness. Then he begins to pray in earnest for God to change his heart because that is where he hoards his selfish desires.

Whatever the time-table for change, when one sincerely wants to be right with God, attitudes and desires are altered as the Holy Spirit teaches the child of God what to want. Years ago when I couldn't find a publisher for my books God taught me the importance of desiring what *He* wants. I knew God could provide a publisher whenever it pleased Him, so I laid my desire before Him and left it there. I continued to pray for His will, but I stopped worrying about the result because I knew His will would be done anyway—in *His* time and in His unique (and always better) way. As I spent more time in God's Word, I came to know Him more intimately. As I learned more about my Heavenly Father, His love for me, and His desire for me to live my life in the fullness of Christ, I felt absolute assurance of two things: Either my books would be published, or they wouldn't! My peace came from knowing that either way, *God was in control..* I was fully aware that I might suffer disappointment, but I knew enough about God to know that He would never leave me or forsake me. If and when I needed comfort, His Holy Spirit would be my Comforter.

I had written the books with a single motive: to share the Person and love of Jesus Christ with children. Because of the strong gospel message in each story, I felt confident that the Lord would use the books to expand His kingdom and through that, He would be glorified. Because I read Scripture faithfully, I knew it would *delight* the Lord to be glorified so there was no reason (at least none that was obvious to me) that He would *not* answer my prayer. As I read God's Word daily, I slowly gained a quiet, solid assurance that the books would eventually be published.

A few of my friends knew that I was writing but I began to tell more people, thinking that doing so would be a great way to challenge myself spiritually, and by voicing my prayer I was sharing my confidence in God. Publication of the books would prove to others that He is faithful to those who study, pray, and persevere. If the books *weren't* published, I would have an opportunity to show how a Christian can continue to love and glorify God, even when He doesn't give us what we want!

It seems strange to me now, but given my extreme confidence in God's ability to give me the desires of my heart, I was not at all anxious for anything to happen. As weeks and months went by I anticipated how I would celebrate God when I received my acceptance letter. But I also anticipated how others might benefit from my disappointment if things did not go the way I hoped they would. I repeat: in my anticipation I was never anxious; I felt perfect peace. I mention that only to give God the glory because the peace I enjoyed was not the result of any effort on my part. It came supernaturally and was only possible because of God's Spirit in me. As peace and common sense prevailed, I reasoned that I had waited over three years; I could wait three-times-three more if that is what God decided.

As I waited, I truly learned to delight in the Lord for who He is. As I studied the attributes of the One True God I gained (for the first time in my life) the peace that surpasses all understanding. I gained hope in God's promise that He wanted me to have abundant life (John 10:10). I learned that whatever happens, God's grace is sufficient, *always* (2 Corinthians 12:9). God would complete the good work He began in me (Philippians 1:6). I can do all things through Him who strengthens me (Philippians 4:13). God is able to establish me by the proclamation of Jesus Christ (Romans 16:25). Through God's Word I came to know—*absolutely*—that my God would never give me such confidence and hope and then disappoint me (Romans 5:5). I also learned that perseverance produces character (Romans 5:4), so I prayed for the strength of heart not to give up!

I accumulated ninety-six rejection letters before the Lord determined that I was spiritually ready for Him to answer my prayer. But when He answered He gave (as He often does) *over and above* anything I had asked for: *Two* of my books were published at the same time by one of the most distinguished Christian publishing houses in America, and both were honored by inclusion on the list of *The Best Christian Children's Books* .

I relay that story not to boast, but to illustrate God's faithfulness to all who claim His promises. I consider myself blessed to recognize my complete inadequacy to do anything apart from Christ. If I have accomplished anything because of the gifts and talents God has so graciously given me, to *Him* be the glory! What I did, is make choices: Using the free will God gave me, I chose to believe His promises, to trust in His faithfulness, to obey Him, to study His word, and to wait for Him to act *according to His will*. I believe God provided the desire of my heart because I sought after Him and that is what delights Him.

## Working Things Out

If you are convinced that the thing you desire will further God's Kingdom, be encouraged to continue in prayer *no matter how long it takes*. But do not allow discontent to obstruct your view of the Lord because God may have a *better* plan. If you have done all the right things and you still do not get what you want, perhaps God is trying to teach you that you must cease striving and know that He is God (Psalm 46:10). Perhaps He is telling you to acknowledge and be content with what He has already given you.

| | |
|---|---|
| *The lot is cast into the lap, but its every decision is from the Lord.*<br>**Proverbs 16:33 (NIV)** | *The lot is cast into the lap; but the whole disposing thereof is of the Lord.*     **(KJV)** |

When we are feeling the most frustrated, we must remember that God is present in the midst of our frustration. At such times we must choose to rest peacefully in His ability to comfort, strengthen and teach us. If we surrender to frustration and allow it to turn into anger, our emotions will almost always distract us from the thing the Lord wants to teach us. Hebrews 12:15 cautions: *"See to it that no one misses the grace of God and that no bitter root grows up to cause trouble..."* In other words, do not fail to take hold of God's grace. If you do not remember God's grace in times of trial your discontent may turn to anger and you will be of no use to anyone!

When we recognize the approach of discontent we must ask God to give us eyes that see clearly and hearts that desire His will—even if His will differs from ours. Patience is its own reward. When perseverance finishes its work, we are left mature and complete, not lacking anything (James 1:4). But patience without peace is a hollow victory. Those who grumble and complain as they wait dishonor the name of God. But those who continue to trust in the Lord (those who *rest peacefully in His will*) become like Mount Zion, which cannot be shaken and endures forever (Psalm 125:1). Those who endure trials and disappointment patiently will reign with Christ and be counted worthy of the kingdom of God for which they have suffered (2 Timothy 2:12, 2 Thessalonians 1:5). Those who remain content in the Lord in spite of adversity will receive the crown of life (Revelation 2:10).

# Life Application: Chapter Three

## Day One:
Read Psalm 104 today and record your thoughts:
After reading this Psalm, what thoughts do you have about God?




## Day Two:
Read Luke 12:29-31. What does this Scripture say about "pagans"?



What is Christ's instruction to the followers of the One True God? V.31



List some of the things that pagans *and* Christians "run after:"



Study your list. What are *you* "running after?"



If Jesus were sitting with you, what do you think He would say about your list?



## Day Three:
Read Colossians 1:1-2. What do you think it means *specifically*, to "set your mind on things above?"

Make a list what you consider to be "earthly things" and "Heavenly things."

**Earthly Things**                              **Heavenly Things**

Of the "earthly things" you listed, on which do you place the most emphasis, and why?

Which of the "Heavenly things" will you give more attention to in order to insure that your perspective on *earthly* things is right before God in the future?

**Day Four:**
Read Psalm 73:21-28. What do these verses say to you regarding God's perspective on the desires of your heart?

Why do you think that many Christians desire earthly things more than Heavenly things?


List some things you can do to guard your heart so that you do not find yourself in bondage to earthly desires.


**Day Five:**
Read 1 Timothy 6:6-10. How will you apply the wisdom in these verses to your life?


What has the Holy Spirit taught you this week about the desires of your heart?


What action will you take to fulfill the desire of your heart?

Chapter 4

# At Peace With God's Provision

*...Give me neither poverty nor riches, but give me only my daily bread. Otherwise, I may have too much and disown you and say "Who is the Lord?"*
**Proverbs 30:8-9 (NIV)**

*Resign every forbidden joy; restrain every wish that is not referred to God's will; banish all eager desires, all anxiety; desire only the will of God; seek Him alone and supremely, and you will find peace.*
**– Archbishop Francis Fenelon**

John D. Rockerfeller, founder of the Standard Oil Company, was the richest man in the world at the time of his death in the early 1900s. At his retirement, a reporter asked Mr. Rockerfeller how much money was "enough?" Rockerfeller responded, "a little bit *more.*"

A desire is something we want—something we believe we need in order to find happiness and contentment. The things we desire reveal much about us because the pursuit of those desires will determine how we spend our precious and limited time on earth. For example, if I already have all I need to survive (food, shelter, and clothing) yet I choose to work exhaustively in order to buy luxuries, I make a clear statement to my family regarding my priorities. If my desire for professional success is so strong that I will compromise or disregard God's Law in order to succeed, I demonstrate to all who know me that my convictions are nothing more than words.

God gave each individual the free will to choose his own desires. Unfortunately, many choose without prayerfully considering the possible consequences of getting what they want. Those who make life-altering choices without prayerfully bringing their desires before God will often choose wrongly and then suffer for their lack of diligence. When we do not seek God first, we often end up wanting the wrong things.

People who desire wrong things and do not get what they want are usually discontented and anxious. Ironically, even when they *do* get what they want they are still discontented and anxious because the thing they wanted was wrong to begin with. Conversely, those who desire only what glorifies God will live in peace as they wait hopefully for Him to provide.

We are conditioned by our culture to believe that if we just have more things we will be content. Advertising executives are paid huge sums of money to convince us that what we already have is not good enough; we need *new* and *improved*. Some blame their discontent on other people: Those who are not married often wish they were, and those who are married often wish they weren't. In that case, one's spouse may become his/her excuse for discontent. Some couples who do not have children want them, and others who have them wish they didn't! Those who have jobs often want a better one so they can earn more money to buy a better car or a bigger home. Some who get promoted may wish they had less responsibility and more leisure time to enjoy the things they've bought. In other words, few of God's creatures are ever *really* content.

The more we dwell on the things we *desire*, the less time we spend praising God for what we already have. The more time we spend working to get the things we want, the less time we spend in sacrificial service to the Lord. Discontent can become a virus grown out of desires that put our wants before our needs and our "self" before our Lord. If we are not careful about what we desire, the virus of discontent will keep us spiritually bedridden and ineffectual for the Kingdom of God.

*Then he said to them, "Watch out! Be on your guard against all kinds of greed; a man's life does not consist in the abundance of his possessions."*    **Luke 12:15 (NIV)**    *And he said unto them, Take heed, and beware of covetousness: for a man's life consisteth not in the abundance of the things which he possesseth.*    **(KJV)**

The desire to possess more "things" is the motivating force that propels many women out of the home and into the work place. Sadly, many Christians have unwittingly fallen prey to the "prosperity" theology preached in pulpits all across America today. The teaching that any child of God can "name-it-and-claim-it" ("it" being material wealth) is a brutal distortion of God's Word. The "abundant life" that Jesus brought does not imply monetary wealth; it refers to *spiritual* wealth: the abundance of peace and contentment manifest only through the unsearchable riches of life in Christ.

Over half of the thirty-six parables of Christ deal with man's attitude toward money. In fact, the New Testament makes more references to money and material possessions than it does to Heaven and Hell combined. Clearly, Jesus understood the force behind money and its ability to pull man away from God.

Sociologists have also recognized the existence of man's problem with money. Since the inception of behavior polls, "money" or "finances" has consistently been identified as the number one cause of marital discord and ultimately, divorce. The love of money—or worry that we won't have enough of it—is volatile fuel for the sins of idolatry, greed, and *discontent*. As Timothy warns, more people fall into sin because of the love of money than for any other reason (1 Timothy 6:10). Perhaps more than any test God gives, man's attitude toward material possessions will establish his character and indicate his degree of spiritual maturity in other areas.

## When You're Doing Things Right, But They're Turning Out Wrong

Bill and Melissa, both devout Christians, owned a successful construction company in the Midwest. The economy soured just as Bill was in the midst of the most lucrative construction project of his career. When his employer couldn't pay him for the work he'd completed, Bill had no money to pay his suppliers. In an effort to accumulate funds, he and Melissa agreed to buy a smaller home, using the equity from their larger home to repay some of their business debts. For months, Bill struggled in vain to find independent contracting jobs, stretching his equity dollars as far as he could. By the time the equity was gone, additional business and personal debts had accumulated. Bill did not consider bankruptcy a viable option for a Christian, so he set up payment schedules with all his creditors. For the next eight years, Bill and Melissa struggled to repay their debts.

Now Melissa says, "When I look back, I think we did all the right things. We both walked with the Lord. We read God's Word daily and we attended worship regularly. We prayed over every business decision we made, and we always sought counsel from other Christians. Still, none of the choices we made provided any monetary compensation. We lost almost everything, but mercifully we managed to hang on to our little house until we could sell it and move into an apartment. Shortly after that, God delivered us from the financial burden.

"It seems like an eternity, looking back on it now. Little by little, we lost all the extras: The summer home, the boat, the extra car, the country club membership.... even most of my jewelry. God took it all..."

She smiles and shakes her head gently, awed at the ways of God: "...I think it's incredible how He took all the frills away, but in His mercy, left us with all the necessities. In all that time, we never missed a house payment, but we came awfully close a couple of times! We never went without food on the table either, and we managed to keep up with the children's tuition. I don't know how we did it, but by God's grace, we did.

"Now Bill has a great job, but I don't think we'll ever return to the lifestyle we lived before. Instead of a country club, we support some missionaries in our church. Instead of a new car, we bought a used van. We fill it with food and clothing for the homeless, and we load it with kids when the youth group goes camping. Instead of owning a second home, we're working to pay off this one. In other words, when we spend money *this* time, we're trying to do it based solely upon the principles given in the Bible. After all, it's *God's* money!

"Our non-Christian friends couldn't believe that we could lose so much *stuff*, and not be devastated. Everything we touched, every idea we had to make money, turned to dust until it all blew away and just the bare necessities were left. But instead of feeling sorry for ourselves, we began to feel convicted about how much we had squandered. God had taken so much, and we still had so much left. We slowly began to see that the less we had materially, the more we thought about God and how much we need to depend on Him to get through each day.

"We've learned to be content with a lot less, and I can't explain how *freeing* that is. There is less to worry about, less to take care of and more time to devote to our family. We both thank God for allowing this financial crisis in our lives. We are grateful that we only had to suffer financially in order to get back on track with God. Our family is physically healthy and as I have indicated, we never really suffered; we never went hungry or worse, homeless. Through it all, Bill and I grew even closer. The experience gave us a whole new perspective on things. Now that we're less concerned with the temporal, we focus more on the *eternal*."

## Divine Intervention vs. Human Diligence

Lack of peace is sometimes the result of the believer's failure to do everything within his power to change things. God's sovereignty does not relieve man of his own responsibility to be diligent in prayer and to seek wise counsel during times of difficulty. The Christian prays because he believes in God's ability to answer his prayers and deliver him from trouble. If he didn't believe God would respond, there would be no reason for him to pray. Unfortunately, many of us pray only when we have exhausted all other efforts to resolve things on our own, when we fail in our attempts to "fix" things, or when others are unable to solve a dilemma for us. Prayer should be our *first* resort because it is through prayer that the Spirit of God instructs and guides us:

*Show me your ways, O Lord, teach me your paths; guide me in your truth and teach me, for you are God my Savior, and my hope is in you all day long.*
### Psalm 25:4-5 (NIV)

*Show me thy ways, O Lord, teach me thy paths. Lead me in thy truth, and teach me: for thou art the God of my salvation; on thee do I wait all the day.* **(KJV)**

We must never forget that God allows Satan to rule the earth on which we stand. Though Satan can do nothing apart from God's will, God allows him to test us. The devil loves to hurl temptation our way by challenging our integrity. Because he is so deceptive, he often throws what we cannot see coming. For example, when one is struggling financially, Satan may (and almost always does) present opportunities for the believer to fall into sin. It can be something as small as a cashier's error in ringing up a purchase, or something as serious as a business opportunity that may not be *illegal,* but isn't exactly forthright. It may be the temptation to cheat on one's income tax, or a reluctance to repay a small personal loan. Such temptations are subtle and attractive. We often seek the most immediate solution to a problem because none of us likes to feel uncomfortable. Satan identifies this Achilles heel in all of us and knows that the most immediate solution to any financial problem is usually the most worldly one.

In the fourth chapter of Matthew, when Satan urges Jesus to use His power to meet His material need for food, Jesus responds by saying: *"It is written: 'Man does not live on bread alone, but on every word that comes from the mouth of God.'"* Christ is our example, and He always placed His commitment to doing the will of God before His physical needs. If we wish to follow His example, we must remain close to the Heavenly Father during times of financial crisis, reading His Word daily and seeking guidance from Him. And we must do so with open minds—setting aside what *we* want and being willing to accept what *God* wants for us.

We rob ourselves of the opportunity to experience God's creativity when we enter into Bible study or prayer with our minds already made up regarding what we think the outcome should be. Very often, the thing we *think* will make us content will not bring us peace at all; we only *think* it will because of our limited imaginations. God is truly the Greatest Visionary, and He has solutions to life's problems that you and I are not capable of dreaming! Because He created us, God knows our strengths and weaknesses better than we do. Because His desire is for our sanctification, His Divine priorities are different from human ones and He often points us in directions we never thought of going. When we do God's will out of simple obedience—*even when we can't imagine the outcome*—He always crowns our efforts with success. Remember however, that God's definition of success is very different from that of the world.

If we have prayed about financial concerns, searched the Scriptures, and still have no clear direction, it is wise to seek counsel from godly men and women. *Godly* counsel comes from one who *knows God's Word* and *makes Christ the example* for his or her life:

*My eyes will be on the faithful in the land, that they may dwell with me; he whose walk is blameless will minister to me.*
**Psalm 101:6 (NIV)**

*Mine eyes shall be upon the faithful of the land, that they may dwell with me; he that walketh in a perfect way, he shall serve me.* **(KJV)**

*For lack of guidance a nation falls, but many advisors make victory sure.* **Proverbs 11:14 (NIV)**

*Where no counsel is, the people fall: but in the multitude of counselors there is safety.* **(KJV)**

A godly counselor will always speak the truth in love, even when the truth is not what the one seeking advice wants to hear. First Kings 22:5-9 presents such an example. Jehoshaphat (king of Judah) agreed to go to war to help Israel, but he advised the king of Israel to "seek the counsel of the Lord" before entering battle. The king responded by gathering four hundred pagan prophets who only proclaimed messages designed to please him. Apparently, the king did not really desire the *Lord's* counsel. Instead, he wanted to hear from those who agreed with him. Sometimes we are like that king. We seek answers from those who will tell us what we want to hear. Or we ask God to put His stamp of approval on our plans without even considering whether the thing we want to accomplish is what God wants for us. When Jehoshaphat recognized the king's counselors as unreliable he asked the king to find a *real* prophet of the Lord. In other words, Jehoshaphat seemed to be saying that *one man with godly wisdom is worth more than four hundred without it!*

At Jehoshaphat's suggestion, I imagine the king lowered his eyes because he responded rather sheepishly: "Well, there *is* one prophet... but I don't like him much because he never prophesies anything good about me!"

He was talking about Micaiah, the prophet of God. You see, even though Micaiah's counsel was full of wisdom, the king ignored him because he didn't tell the king what he wanted to hear. But Jehoshaphat insisted, so the king reluctantly acquiesced and sent a messenger for Micaiah.

By the time Micaiah arrived, the prophesying had already begun. A spokesman for the four hundred had already instructed the king to take up iron horns and gore the Arameans until they were all destroyed. He promised the king that he would be victorious, so naturally the other three hundred and ninety-nine "yes men" concurred. As Micaiah and the messenger approached the thrones of the kings, the messenger filled Micaiah in on what had previously taken place. He told Micaiah how the others had prophesied and advised him to agree with them. After all, four hundred prophets couldn't *all* be wrong! Knowing full well the consequences that could result from his own dissidence, Micaiah still responded by saying, "As surely as the Lord lives, I can tell [the king] only what the Lord tells me." (v.14)

The story of Micaiah and the king of Israel is an excellent example of biblical accountability. Christians owe it to one another to tell the truth in love—regardless of the consequences—even though the truth is often painful to the one who hears it. If you are discontented with the circumstances in which the Lord has allowed you to live, God can use others to help you see the areas in your life where spiritual growth is needed.

We must persevere and remain diligent during times of financial adversity. Once we have prayed, listened for God's direction, and sought godly counsel, we are called to use all means available to us—*as long as those means are pleasing to God and do not violate any of His commands*—-in order to affect a change in our situation. For example, we cannot expect God to provide a job for us if we are not willing to actively seek employment. And we cannot expect someone to hire us if we show up late for a job interview or present ourselves in an unprofessional way. God receives no glory from lazy men and women. To sit around and wait for God to act on our behalf is a disgrace to the One who gives us the physical and mental ability to do His will. Solomon makes that quite clear in the Proverbs:

*Go to the ant, you sluggard; consider its ways and be wise! It has no commander, no overseer or ruler, yet it stores its provisions in summer and gathers its food at*

*Go to the ant, thou sluggard; consider her ways, and be wise: Which having no guide, overseer, or ruler, Provideth her meat in the summer, and gathereth her food in the har-*

*harvest. How long will you lie there, you sluggard? When will you get up from your sleep? A little sleep, a little slumber, a little folding of the hands to rest – and poverty will come on you like a bandit and scarcity like an armed man.*
**Proverbs 6:6-11 (NIV)**

*vest. How long wilt thou sleep, O sluggard? when wilt thou arise out of thy sleep? Yet a little sleep, a little slumber, a little folding of the hands to sleep: So shall thy poverty come as one that travelleth, and thy want as an armed man.*
**(KJV)**

In summary, there are specific things the Christian must do to experience peace during times of financial (or any other) adversity:

- Pray diligently
- Read Scripture daily
- Wait and *listen* for God's response
- If clarification is needed, seek counsel from godly men and women
- Use all means available to you to change your situation, as long as those means glorify God
- And finally, *no matter how badly you want something*, remember: *God will never lead you to do anything that violates or even slightly compromises His holy and perfect law.*

## How God Responds

Unfortunately, the desires of the flesh can interfere with our ability to pray for God's will. Sometimes we want what we want for purely selfish reasons—reasons that may prove to be harmful to us. From His omniscient (all-knowing) vantage point, God sees every possible scenario associated with each requested prayer. And because He knows the *true* motivation behind each petition—and the consequences that will result if He responds the way *we* want—He often answers in ways we don't expect.

The desires of our hearts (and the world in general) may cloud our vision in such a way that we cannot see the possible spiritual damage, should God give us what we think we want. When praying about matters of finance, be aware that God often responds in the following ways:

1. *God may reveal that a specific area of sin in your life has contributed to your circumstances.* In matters of finance, the sins are often greed or covetousness, which lead to poor stewardship of God's assets. Once the sin is confessed and the sinner repentant, God will begin to work things out.

2. *God may answer your prayer by opening doors that set you on a course completely different from what you expected.* For example, one who is unemployed may be offered a lower paying job, or employment in a completely different field from the one for which he has trained. Such an answer may require relocation or a drastic change in lifestyle, but these things move him closer to God if he is willing to submit and make a change based on faith.

3. *God may reveal altogether new possibilities in order to move you toward a solution.* While we may view a problem as purely financial, that may be only a surface result of a much deeper need we can't see. God always sees problems *and* solutions in their entirety and through prayer and counsel with others, He often presents us with creative ways to solve problems for which there seem to be no solution.

"We were praying for money," BethAnn said. "Rick had been out of work for eighteen months and we had no medical insurance. Our daughter, Holly had a skiing accident about a year before and she was having trouble with her knees and needed surgery. Not only could we not afford that, but most of her college fund had been used for living expenses. Rick finally found another job, but he took a cut in pay. Specifically, we were praying about whether or not Rick should take a second job. Neither of us wanted that; he was already working over fifty hours a week in order to get overtime pay. I know this sounds stupid, but it never even *occurred* to Rick or me that *I* could get a job. I hadn't worked outside our home since our first child was born.

"After we prayed a few days, I ran into an old friend of ours who owns a small business. His office manager had quit suddenly and he was in desperate need of someone. The job required filing, phone answering and typing skills—all of which I had, but it also required some basic computer skills I didn't have. Even so, he offered me the job and half jokingly offered to train me.

"After I got home, I began to think about it. Holly was the last child at home and she was going off to college in a few months. I was already having trouble with that, dreading the thought of being home alone all day long. We have raised five children and I haven't been really *alone* for twenty-three years! All my time has been spent with them, at school, sporting events, dance recitals, youth group. The more I thought about it, the idea of working again was appealing to me, even though I didn't feel very confident about entering the work force. Rick and I talked about it and he thought it was a great idea; there was really no reason for me *not* to take the job and besides the extra income, I got full medical benefits immediately, which is really unusual.

"I have been there almost two years and I *love* my job. I've learned new skills, the job is interesting and challenging, and I've made some great new friends. Since then, Rick's found a better job and is back to full salary. I could quit working, but I like it."

In His wisdom and creativity, the Lord made a way for BethAnn and Rick to solve their financial problems, enriching BethAnn's life and easing her loneliness in the process. BethAnn expressed some reservations at first, but she recognized the job as an answer to prayer because the income would produce the extra money they needed to supplement Holly's education and pay their medical bills as well. The job didn't interfere with her duties as wife and mother, and she had her husband's approval. In other words, both partners agreed, so both felt God's peace with the decision.

Although we have a responsibility to do everything we can to change our situation, we must be content with the reality that our situation may never change. Those who have had much may have to learn to be content with little, and those who have had little, may be forced to get along with less. Whatever one's financial situation, faith in God's sovereignty and His desire for all His children to experience abundant life, are the keys to contentment in the area of finances.

*I am not saying this because I am in need, for I have learned to be content whatever the circumstances. [12] I know what it is to*

*Not that I speak in respect of want: for I have learned, in whatsoever state I am, therewith to be content. [12] I know both how to be abased,*

*be in need, and I know what it is to have plenty. I have learned the secret of being content in any and every situation, whether well fed or hungry, whether living in plenty or in want. [13] I can do everything through him who gives me strength.*

*and I know how to abound: every where and in all things I am instructed both to be full and to be hungry, both to abound and to suffer need. [13] I can do all things through Christ which strengtheneth me.            (KJV)*

*Philippians. 4:11-13 (NIV)*

## Life Application: Chapter Four

### Day One:

Read the following Scriptures and be prepared to discuss what these verses tell you regarding God's viewpoint on money.

1 Chronicles 29:11-12

Deuteronomy 8:17-18

### Day Two:

Read 1 Timothy 4:6-7 and record what it says:

In what area(s) of your life do you find it most difficult to submit to God? Give the question serious thought before you record your response. Record all areas in which you have a problem with submission.

Consider your response, above. *If* you *choose* to submit to God, how do you think He might change your situation?

Read Philippians 4:11-13. How do you think one can *learn* to be content?

**Day Three:**
Read Matthew 6:28-34 and record your understanding the verses:
Why is it a sin to worry about finances?

What are you telling others about your faith in God if they know you are constantly worried about money or seeking after possessions?

**Day Four:**
Read and meditate upon Proverbs 30:8-9. What are some ways in which having "too much" can cause us to disown the Lord?

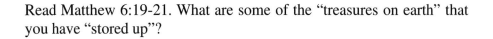

Read Matthew 6:19-21. What are some of the "treasures on earth" that you have "stored up"?

List some of the treasures that you can "store up for heaven:"

**Day Five:**
Read Psalm 17:15. According to this verse, what should bring us contentment each day when we wake up?

Read Job 1:21. How do you think Job viewed his possessions, his children, and his own life?

Ask God to reveal to you the truth about how you view your finances. Record what you believe He has told you:

How do you think God would like your attitude about money to change?

# Chapter 5

# Peace,
# Whatever Your
# Circumstances

*The Lord Almighty has sworn, "Surely, as
I have planned, so it will be, and as I have
purposed, so it will stand."*
**Isaiah 14:24 (NIV)**

*Submission is the only reasoning between
a creature and its Maker and contentment
in his will is the best remedy we can apply
to misfortunes.* **– Sir William Temple**

Doug buried his head in his hands; it was all he could do to keep from crying. For the third time, he had been passed over for a promotion. While his boss admitted that Doug was most deserving, the "powers-that-be" had decided that his eighteen years with the company and his impeccable performance record could not compensate for his age; they had decided to go with a younger man....

For almost seven years, Christi and Joe have prayed for a child. They have spent thousands of dollars on specialists and hundreds of hours in prayer. Still they remain childless....

The family watched in horror and disbelief as the casket containing the body of their only son was lowered into the ground. They were no longer faced with the task of choosing between the professional baseball contract or the Princeton scholarship; both dreams, like smoke in the wind, had disappeared....

The young woman sat alone in her room, her wedding gown draped over the back of a chair. She had been trying for several hours to stop crying, but she couldn't. Her shock and dismay were only the beginning; she still had to contend with the humiliation of returning all the gifts and telling everyone that the wedding was off. The man she loved was going to marry someone else and there was nothing she could say or do to make him change his mind.

*"For I know the plans I have for you," declares the Lord, "plans to prosper you and not to harm you, plans to give you hope and a future."* **Jeremiah 29:11 (NIV)**

*For I know the thoughts that I think toward you, saith the Lord, thoughts of peace, and not of evil, to give you an expected end.* **(KJV)**

The goals we set for ourselves indicate to God and to others what is really important to us. It seems so natural to desire worldly things that to most people, it seems *un*natural to desire the things of God. We often set goals based upon what the *world* says we need; seldom do we list a desire to "Do the will of God" as our first priority. By contrast, Jesus, our example, had a single desire during His lifetime among men. His first priority was to obey God by doing His will, and every effort Jesus expended was directed toward the fulfillment of that singular goal.

Disappointment that stems from frustrated dreams is always self-centered; we are unhappy because we do not get what we want, when and under the conditions we want it. We can avoid frustration if we simply believe that the Lord will do what He promises. Regardless of our situation, God promises that *all* grace abounds to us. He does not say, *"I give grace enough to survive—unless you don't get that promotion."* He doesn't promise grace sufficient to see us through anything *"except financial failure,"* and he doesn't promise abundant life *"...unless of course, you remain childless or become ill."*

We see the things we desire from a human perspective. The one who desires a promotion cannot always see that the job he wants may cause him to compromise his Christian values. The one who wants more money cannot always know that possessions may have a negative effect on him spiritually. And more seriously, the family that loses a child or the person suffering with a chronic or terminal illness cannot possibly see the end result of their witness to others. But *God sees everything*.

*I rejoice greatly in the Lord that at last you have renewed your concern for me. Indeed, you have been concerned, but you had no opportunity to show it. I am not saying this because I am in need, for I have learned to be content whatever the circumstances. I know what it is to be in need, and I know what it is to have plenty. I have learned the secret of being content in any and every situation, whether well fed or hungry, whether living in plenty or in want. I can do everything through him who gives me strength.* **Philippians 4:10-13**

*But I rejoiced in the Lord greatly, that now at the last your care of me hath flourished again; wherein ye were also careful, but ye lacked opportunity. Not that I speak in respect of want: for I have learned, in whatsoever state I am, therewith to be content. I know both how to be abased, and I know how to abound: every where and in all things I am instructed both to be full and to be hungry, both to abound and to suffer need. I can do all things through Christ which strengtheneth me.* **(KJV)**

The enemy feeds on our discontent, as evidenced by the biblical story of Eve. Our dissatisfaction is one of the things that energizes Satan most. If he can keep us disappointed with God and focused on the things we consider unfair, he can keep us weak and vulnerable to the sins of self-pity, anxiety and discontent. When a Christian feels discouraged because he cannot have what he wants, he must be quick to discern the difference between happiness and contentment. Happiness depends upon external circumstances (getting what you want), but the peace of God is *internal* and not dependent upon the outwardly visible. It is the result of the believer's hope in Christ. Once the believer understands the hope that comes only from Jesus, peace is a soft pillow upon which his soul rests. Hope in the Lord revives those who have it. Hope gives the believer the energy he needs to keep on going, no matter how long it takes.

It is possible for Christians to feel victoriously content, even when personal goals and desires go unrealized. Even as the enemy whispers, *"You failed! You'll never be happy now!"* the Christian can experience contentment in the midst of disappointment by viewing frustrated goals from an eternal perspective: If the thing we want does not glorify God, help us or others grow spiritually, or increase God's Kingdom, it is not worthy of our attention when viewed from an eternal perspective. While the Lord can and does frustrate the goals of men, *He will never allow goals set in accordance with His will to fail!* In setting the goals and priorities that will define your life, the way to know the will of God is to communicate with Him daily and to know and believe His Word.

## When God's Desires Become Ours

As a childless widow in her mid-thirties, Betsy enjoyed a lucrative career. She had been with the same agency since graduating from college and after ten years, she controlled four of the agency's six biggest accounts. Her boss was impressed with her charm and ability, and her co-workers assumed she was on her way to becoming a partner in the firm. Betsy thrived on the demanding nature and frantic pace of her job because it always challenged her creativity. On her climb to the top of the corporate ladder, she had always acknowledged the Lord, continually praying for His guidance and then thankfully acknowledging His blessings.

Though she loved her job, Betsy worked in an industry that often compromised her Christian values. Her boss pushed her to pad expenditures and deceive clients, but she refused to do it. One day he threatened her, insisting that if she didn't lie to a client's wife, she would lose her job. When she stood her ground, she was fired.

"I didn't understand at first," she admits. "It was totally...*frustrating!* I knew I had done the right thing by not compromising, so I could not understand why the Lord didn't provide a job for me right away. I was unemployed for almost six months; I couldn't find *anything.* I finally got a job at a small independent agency but I had to take a huge cut in pay; I made enough to pay my bills but there was nothing left at the end of the month. The medical coverage wasn't very good, so I began to worry that I might get sick. And I worried about my retirement. I'm only thirty-five, but I'm a *widow;* I have to think about those things." She shrugs her shoulders, smiling. "I know it's a sin to worry, but I'm only human. And really, I only worried for a while. Then God reminded me that these were *His* problems, not mine. I knew that eventually He would intervene and until He did, all I could do was be patient, keep praying, and be content with the situation until He moved to change it.

"A few months ago I was offered a better paying job. I was tempted to take it because of the money but it was in an entirely different field, and not really what I wanted. So I turned it down and continued to pray. I understand now how foolish it was not to take that job, but I never dreamed it would take me so long to get another offer. I prayed *constantly* about that circumstance because I couldn't understand what God was trying to teach me through it. I had sincerely asked God to search my heart. Was there sin I had not confessed? Was He withholding blessing from me until I recognized it? Or maybe my motivation was wrong? I didn't *think* I was asking for too much. I had just lost my husband; I needed a job that paid well and had benefits. But what if I didn't get that? Would I be able to accept God's will if He allowed me to lose everything material, too? Was He testing me to see how I would handle *that*? What was He trying to teach me? As I said, I prayed constantly. I *really* sought after God; *I wanted to know*.. During that time He never revealed any unconfessed sin to me. He never convicted me of any wrong motivation, either. He *did* convict me of a couple of things though: I admitted to Him that I was still too weak from losing Kevin; I didn't think that I could stand losing the home we had shared, too. I remember praying, *I know it's yours, Lord. But if you have to take it, will you just wait until I'm stronger? I just don't think I can handle it now...*

"You see, in my mind, I had reached my limit physically and emotionally. I know that God never gives us more than we can bear; whatever happens, He *will* uphold us. But at that time I was emotionally exhausted and I had convinced myself that I could *not* handle the stress of being forced to sell our home and move. I confessed that I was holding on tight but right now, I just did not have the emotional ability to let go of the memories Kevin and I had shared there. And you know what? After admitting that to God, He gave me that *peace that surpasses all understanding*. It was comfort like a warm, soft blanket on a cold night; God comforted me with the verse in Matthew that says, *a bruised reed he will never break....* When I thought about that, I knew that my Lord would never use adversity to break me. *Whatever* happened, I could handle it.

"Soon after that, God showed me that the job I had turned down had actually been an answer to my prayer. *But because it wasn't the answer I wanted or expected, I had ignored His provision.* As I continued to pray about my circumstance after that, I began to see that the Lord was steering me away from my previous career and into something else. I can't explain it but I began to *hate* the field I thought I loved! Suddenly, I couldn't wait to try something different! Then *this* job came along! In just six months, I'll be making what I made at the big agency, and since I came to work here, I've led two co-workers to the Lord!"

Betsy had not expected God to lead her down a "Blue Highway," but that's exactly what He did. And because she went willingly, He was able to bless her and use her for His glory. Though Betsy's plans were temporarily frustrated, she persevered in prayer and that effort kept her in God's peace while she waited for Him to act on her behalf. Because her desire was always to abide in Christ and obey God's will, He seemed to bless her in a special way: He actually changed the desires of her heart until she was content in a new field where she has done more to glorify Him. Though disappointment often comes through human sources, man's ultimate destiny is always Divinely appointed.

*Now I want you to know, brothers, that what has happened to me has really served to advance the gospel. As a result, it has become clear throughout the whole palace guard and to everyone else that I am in chains for Christ.*
**Philippians. 1:12-13 (NIV)**

*But I would ye should understand, brethren, that the things which happened unto me have fallen out rather unto the furtherance of the gospel; So that my bonds in Christ are manifest in all the palace, and in all other places;* **(KJV)**

*In this you greatly rejoice, though now for a little while you may have had to suffer grief in all kinds of trials. These have come so that your faith—of greater worth than gold, which perishes even though refined by fire—may be proved genuine and may result in praise, glory and honor when Jesus Christ is revealed.* **1 Peter 1:6-7 (NIV)**

*Wherein ye greatly rejoice, though now for a season, if need be, ye are in heaviness through manifold temptations: That the trial of your faith, being much more precious than of gold that perisheth, though it be tried with fire, might be found unto praise and honour and glory at the appearing of Jesus Christ:* **(KJV)**

What Betsy didn't know was that her former boss (the Chief Executive Officer of the company) had been embezzling money. A year-and-a-half after he fired her, he forced the agency into bankruptcy. Thirty-two executives lost their jobs, and all left with no hope of collecting almost three months of back pay and commissions they had earned.

When we are forced to endure circumstances we would rather avoid, we seldom stop to think of all that God protects us from: we take a hard fall but avoid breaking a bone, or (this happened to me) someone runs a red light at fifty miles per hour and *barely* misses hitting our car. Think of the news reports that always follow natural disasters. As the camera scans the rubble that used to be a neighborhood, someone dazed speaks into the reporter's microphone: "My neighbor lost everything, but we didn't have so much as a broken plate...." Sometimes God shields us in ways that are obvious, but we are most often *not* aware of all that He saves us from. I always compare my adversity to Christ's suffering at the cross: Is my cross as heavy? Am I experiencing the degree of humiliation *He* felt? Is the pain I feel as excruciating as the pain of having nails driven through my hands and feet and a sword piercing my side? Does my discomfort even *compare* to what He suffered for me?

Satan has one goal: to destroy God's people. If he can use circumstances to cause us to doubt God's promises, *he wins.* But he cannot win unless we *surrender* to him. *We are God's people.* The enemy cannot touch us without His permission. However, the reality is: *God allows him to touch us.* But in His wisdom and mercy, there is always a divine and refining purpose behind Satan's rude intrusion. And always, *Satan is God's puppet; he can only operate under the sovereign control of his Master's hand.* At will, the Most High God can jerk Satan's strings, yank him from the scene, and stuff him into a suitcase!

People often claim there is "nothing one can do" about difficult circumstances, but there are *always* things we can do: We can ask God to teach us (Psalm 119:71). We can pray without ceasing, praising and thanking Him in *everything* because that is His will for us (1 Thessalonians 5:17-18). We can refuse to give in to fear and doubt, and we can claim the power that is ours through the Spirit of the resurrected Christ (2 Timothy 1:7 and John 3:34). *If we choose to,* we can make every circumstance an opportunity to be taught by God (John 14:26). By willfully submitting to all that God allows, we give Him permission to change us. In other words, when *self* gets out of the way the Holy Spirit has room to work.

When we trust God to do the impossible, feelings of inadequacy turn into feelings of assurance. Fear changes to hopeful anticipation as the peaceful confidence of God seeps into the heart, replacing the anxiety the enemy planted there. When we let God be God, insecurity is quickly and miraculously transformed into boldness as we recognize and acknowledge God's ability to do the impossible in any situation. *That* is why it is possible for any believer who so chooses, to "consider it all joy" in spite of how things look. Whenever we face trials of many kinds, we can know *absolutely* that God's grace is sufficient for us.

While in prison, Paul continued to preach the gospel. In chains, he wrote profound epistles that have encouraged believers throughout centuries and will continue to do so until Christ returns. Paul refused to give in to his circumstances, enabling incalculable numbers of people and nations to benefit from the suffering he *willingly* endured for the sake of Christ. In his Bible commentary on the book of Philippians, Matthew Henry writes (in reference to Paul):

> "Let us leave it to Christ, which way he will make us serviceable to his glory, whether by labour or suffering, by diligence or patience, by living to his honour in working for him, or dying to his honour in suffering for him."[1]

Instead of pitying himself, Paul focused on others. He did more than endure suffering; he was at peace enough to *thank* God in the midst of it. And Paul did not just rise above his circumstances, he *rejoiced* in them— even though he could see no end to his suffering (Philippians 1).

When we are faced with adversity we want to change our circumstances, when God wants to change *us*. There is peace in knowing that God is always in control and that He has the power to free us from whatever chains we are in. But He always frees us in *His* perfect time and *His* perfect (and often creatively- unexpected) way. Therefore, the challenge to *us* lies not in breaking our chains, but in making the most of our time until we are set free.

---

[1] WordSearch Computer Software, Navigators

## Life Application: Chapter Five

### Day One:

Read ECCLESIASTES 7:13-15 and record what the verses teach you about adverse circumstances:

Read Colossians 1:9-12 and list six things Paul prays for all believers:

- 
- 
- 
- 
- 
- 

How does one learn the will of God? V.9

Why is it important for you to know the will of God for your life? V. 10

### Day Two:

Record a specific circumstance in which you lack God's peace right now:

Now, read Proverbs 16:2-3 and answer the following questions:

What do you see as the primary motivation behind your desire to change this circumstance?


How will changing this circumstance glorify God?


How will getting the thing you want help you to grow spiritually?


Will getting the thing you want help to expand the kingdom of God? If so, how?


Do you still think you are right to desire the thing you want?
Explain your answer.


**Day Three:**
Read the following verses and list some of the reasons why believers may lack peace in their lives:

Joshua 7:6-11


Psalm 34:14


Ecclesiastes 4:8

Isaiah 48:17-18


**Day Four:**
Read Isaiah 26:3. What is necessary in order to assure peace in one's life?


What does it mean to you to "be kept in perfect peace?"


How does one keep one's mind "steadfast?"


Read Luke 1:78-79. How does one find the "path of peace?"


What is the implication when Scripture says that God "guides our feet" into the path of peace?


Read Proverbs 3:13-17. What is the destiny of the one who seeks wisdom?

List some practical ways to "seek wisdom" in difficult circumstances:

**Day Five:**
According to the following verses, what will ensure genuine and lasting peace?

John 14:23-27

Romans 5:1-2

Hebrews 12:14

What is the most significant thing you have learned about circumstances?

How has this knowledge changed the way you think?

# Chapter 6

# The Simple Life

*Therefore I tell you, do not worry about your life, what you will eat or drink; or about your body, what you will wear. Is not life more important than food, and the body more important than clothes? Look at the birds of the air; they do not sow or reap or store away in barns, and yet your heavenly Father feeds them. Are you not much more valuable than they?*
**Matthew 6:25-26 (NIV)**

*How are we going to be simple with the simplicity of Jesus? By receiving His Spirit, recognizing and relying on Him, obeying Him as He brings the Word of God, and life will become amazingly simple.* **– Oswald Chambers**

Simplicity means different things to different people. For example, those who have many material possessions may consider cleaning out the closets one way to simplify their lives.

Archbishop Francois Fenelon referred to simplicity as the "pearl of the Gospel." Indeed, Jesus was a simple man. Nothing in Scripture (or in any other historical record) indicates that He owned anything but the clothes on his back. His only pursuit was *people*. The desire of Jesus was to possess the hearts, souls, and minds of *people*.

The counsel Christ gives is as uncomplicated as the way in which He lived: To all who desire to follow Him He said, quite simply, *"Abide in me..."* Through His death, He offered the simplest possible way to salvation and eternal life: *believe in me and you are saved*. Nothing could be more simple than to simply believe what God says: *"I Am..."*

*God said to Moses, "I AM WHO I AM. This is what you are to say to the Israelites: 'I AM' has sent me to you."* **Exodus 3:14 (NIV)**

*And God said unto Moses, I AM THAT I AM: and he said, Thus shalt thou say unto the children of Israel, I AM has sent me unto you.* **(KJV)**

By referring to Himself as *I AM,* God reveals His existence and unchangeable nature. The Almighty God did not come into being by some external source. The Holy One of Israel was, is, and always will be. God Most High exists outside of time and change; He is dependable, faithful, and trustworthy. He is the "God of our fathers"—a designation that speaks of His desire to have an intimate relationship with every individual He created. Therefore the Creator put into the heart of His creation a desire to be connected to Someone outside of "self." Those who lack peace will find it when they realize the most significant pursuit of men and women is an intimate relationship with the Living God—the source of true peace. If we choose to, we can save the minutes we waste each day and invest them in our relationship with God Most High. Instead of waking with a mind set on a thousand small things, we can choose each day to concentrate on one thing: *knowing God more deeply.* We can take every thought captive to Christ and know that as we fix our eyes on Jesus, He will take care of the details that consume us. For example, instead of worrying about money, we can consider the promise of *Jehovah Jireh: God provides.* Instead of worrying about how we will solve a particular problem, we can ponder the wisdom of God and know that He will show us a solution. Instead of fretting over (what we perceive to be) our inadequacies, we can contemplate the life of Christ and know that as we continue to seek Him, He will mold us into His image.

Just as the quality of our lives is determined by the choices we make, our priorities define the kind of life we will have. Those who opt for a peaceful life must choose to live more simply so they have more time to spend communicating with God. Time is the most precious commodity we have. Unlike money or food, there is no way for *any* of us to know when we will run out of time. Yet sadly, time is what we most frequently squander. Those who believe eternal life is a reality must seriously assess the amount of time they spend in an effort to know the One with whom they will spend eternity.

In spite of all God has done and continues to do (by virtue of His grace) for each of us, we often refuse His peace and opt for worry and busy-ness. We worry that we're not doing enough, or that we're not doing it well enough. We worry that if we don't do such-and-such, So-and-So will be hurt or angry (or both.) So we commit to doing more than we should. Later, we resent both the task *and* the person. We worry that un-expected company will see a mess in the living room or dirty dishes in the sink, so instead of spending a few quiet minutes with the Lord, we rush to clean the house "just in case someone drops by." Most of us think nothing of talking idly on the telephone for twenty minutes, but we "just can't find the time" to read the Bible. In reality, most of us would have peace in our lives if we would simply stop doing so many insignificant things and focus on the one thing that is most important: Our relationship with the Savior.

*Be very careful, then, how you live—not as unwise but as wise, making the most of every opportunity, because the days are evil. Therefore do not be foolish, but understand what the Lord's will is.* **Ephesians. 5:15-17 (NIV)**

*See then that ye walk circumspectly, not as fools, but as wise, Redeeming the time, because the days are evil. Wherefore be ye not unwise, but understanding what the will of the Lord is.* **(KJV)**

I often hear people—particularly women—say that they are going to simplify their lives. They have too much going on (they say) so they are going to cut back on their activities. They are unorganized; they are going to start prioritizing their responsibilities. They have too much "stuff" they say, so they are going to clean out the closets. Those are the things they *say*, but most of them will do nothing to actually change things. To those who truly want peace in their lives, simplicity must be more than a thought; it must be manifest in a changed life where God is one's first priority.

For a moment, imagine yourself walking out of the grocery store carrying two plastic bags. You bought a carton of milk, a dozen eggs, a couple of cantaloupes, a box of cereal, a loaf of bread, a pound of butter, an economy-size jar of peanut butter...and some toothpaste. The contents are too heavy for the flimsy bags, and you can feel the stretch in the handles as the plastic is pulled taut before it stretches so far that it finally *snaps*! You hurriedly gather the bags into your arms, wondering how you will get the car door open if you are blessed enough to make it to the car before tomorrow's breakfast hits the sidewalk!

After taking a couple cautious steps, you feel the eggs sliding between your arm and your hip, toward the sidewalk. When you move quickly to keep them from falling, one of your cantaloupes rolls free and you drop it. When you bend to pick up the first cantaloupe, the *second* one rolls free, followed by the milk! As you fall to your knees, clutching what is left of your groceries, the toothpaste (because it is so small) slips and drops, too. Exasperated, you give up your struggle as everything else topples to the sidewalk. While you kneel there, defeated and ready to cry, a stranger approaches, carrying one of those big, double-strength shopping bags—the kind with *real* handles. Without saying a word, he picks up each item—carefully, one at a time—and places it into the bag. Then he smiles slowly and sweetly, takes your elbow, and without saying a word, gently leads you to your car, carrying the heavy bag for you all the way.

When other things are scattered around us, we must look to Jesus; He will be there to gather them up—to hold everything together. We need not worry about our daily life because He will carry our burdens for us (Matthew 6:25, 1 Peter 5:7). When we find ourselves running frantically in all directions—whether it be to a meeting, the grocery store, a child's soccer game or into the kitchen to prepare dinner, *we must take time out for God.* Those who do not run to Christ will run after other things. The more we have and *do*, the more "cluttered" our lives become. The more bound we become to doing *things*, the less time we have to bind ourselves with God. Jesus warns us to be careful, reminding us that where our treasure is, our hearts will follow (Matthew 6:21). Time is a priceless treasure; that is why Satan wants to snatch it away—particularly when we want to spend that time alone with God. Decide how you will spend your time each day, consider this: minutes and hours spent in the pursuit of material things or consumed with busy-ness are minutes and hours *not spent* with your Heavenly Father.

We cannot ignore the fact that we live in a busy and material world, but we can learn to live in a way that reflects a priority for eternal treasure:

- We can share our time, talents, and money with individuals and organizations devoted to the cause of Christ.
- We can buy only what we *need* and purchase goods for their function, not for their status.
- We can tithe.
- We can save some money for the future and use the abundance God provides to help those in need.
- We can pare down: give away things we don't use and clothes we don't wear.
- We can consider the blessings God has already given us, and ask His forgiveness when we find ourselves yearning for more.
- We can spend less time doing things that do not help expand God's kingdom and *more* time doing things that will. What could be more simple?

Betty, who is sixty-six years old, has been a widow for twelve years. Her husband John died of cancer at the age of fifty-five, just three months after doctors detected the disease. Before his illness, John earned a modest salary as a factory worker. Betty says they never went without the necessities, but jokes that "there was never enough money to buy frosting for the cake." They always maintained a small savings account, but by the time John's funeral expenses were paid, it was gone.

"I was fifty-four when John died," Betty said, "...and I had never worked outside of my home. John and I married when I was seventeen and back then, it never occurred to me to have a career. All I had ever done—all I ever *wanted* to do—was take care of my home and family. To be honest, I was *afraid* to enter the workforce after John died. I didn't have any real skills, so the best I could hope for was a minimum-wage job. So there I was: an unskilled widow at the age of fifty-four!

"John had a life insurance policy, but a few years before he died we cashed it in so that we could send our son to technical school. We had always planned to buy another one, but we never did because the money was always needed for something else—like brakes on the car or a new furnace. If I told you I felt desperate and hopeless, I would be understating the facts.

"After a few months of wringing my hands and worrying about how I would survive, I decided that it was time to start living out the faith I was always talking about. I confessed my sin of worrying and not trusting God, and I asked Him to forgive me. Then I told God that from that day forward, I would trust Him for everything, and I began to pray in earnest for His direction.

"After a few weeks of consistently spending time with God, I felt Him instructing me to sell my house. The house wasn't much, but we had been there for twenty-five years and it was almost paid for. My children were grown and living on their own, so financially I was only responsible for myself. John had always managed the finances, and I was not confident in my own ability to make such a big decision, so I made an appointment with a financial planner who attends my church. After refusing to accept a fee from me for his services, he offered to design a living plan for me.

"I thought that was really quite amazing. I didn't even know the man but he knew about me because he had read about John's death several months earlier in the church bulletin. The first day I saw him, he told me he had been praying for me. Needless to say, I felt blessed. God knew how insecure I was about finances, so He provided help.

"Eleven years ago, I sold the house and bought this little trailer. It's not much, but it's all I need. I made enough money from the sale of the house to pay cash for it, and I still had plenty left over. I put some of the money in a savings account and the rest was invested for me. I get a little money from the investments every three months and with Social Security, I have enough for food and utilities. Since I don't have to hold down a job, I have time to serve at church. I teach Sunday school and lead a women's Bible study on Thursdays. Every other Wednesday, I volunteer at the Crisis Pregnancy Center. I don't have much, but I have a peaceful life."

## The Essential of Simplicity

The essential of simplicity is not complicated: *seek God first.* But most of us find the *method* of minimalism difficult. Scripture tells us not to put too much emphasis on worldly possessions because we cannot serve two masters. Scripture also says that our beliefs about money can be deceptive, causing us to sin (Matthew 6:24, Ecclesiastes 10:19). In other words, we can be deceived into thinking that money is the answer to everything, when it is actually the *cause* of most of the problems we have as individuals and societies. For example, those who think they don't have enough money can feel envious of those who have a lot. And if they feel they deserve more than they have, they may steal, cheat, or lie to get what they want. Conversely, those who have more money than they need usually want more. Some don't care what they do to get it, and they don't think twice about abusing those who get in their way.

On the societal level, government throws money at cultural problems instead of dealing with the sin that causes them. Lawmakers allow government schools to teach that promiscuous sex is acceptable; then when people contract diseases or fear other consequences because of their reckless behavior, government throws money into AIDS research and School Based Clinics that give contraceptives to children. Women who have babies out of wedlock are encouraged with government money to have *more* of them, and people who simply refuse to work have their laziness financially rewarded through welfare programs that keep them comfortable while they do nothing to help themselves. Whether speaking of personal or societal issues, the list of problems we think can be solved with money is exhaustive. The truth is that money won't solve anything until we accept the fact that we are really dealing with sin. Greed and coveting are only symptoms of the real problem: What we think and how we feel about money. Illegitimacy is not the real issue; promiscuity is the issue—sexual sin is the issue. And AIDS is only a consequence of the real problem we face: a perceived "acceptance" of one type of sexual perversion that kills millions of homosexual people who are dearly loved by God.

Jesus did not just talk about loving others. He actively demonstrated His love by what He did—to the point of surrendering all at the cross. As with every spiritual discipline, simplicity is a matter of obedience and submission. It is the result of one's internal motivation and desire to imitate Christ by unselfishly serving others: *I will spend less time thinking about what I want, and more time considering the needs of others... I will purchase less for myself because God has given me so much. I will bless others by sharing the blessings God has given me; in that way, He will be glorified.... I will spend less time chasing after things, and more time serving those in need.... I will move out of my comfort zone; for once, I will step out of the air conditioning and into the heat of battle.*

We need not worry whether God will give us "enough," because He promises to provide what we need (Philippians 4:19). We need not wonder whether He will be there when we need Him because He has already promised that He will be (Hebrews 13:5). We need not fear inadequacy because His Holy Spirit will enable us (Philippians 4:13).

In his wonderful book, *The Pursuit of God,* A.W. Tozer writes:

"Our woes began when God was forced out of His central shrine [the human heart] and *things* were allowed to enter.... Men have now by nature no peace within their hearts, for God is crowned there no longer.... God's gifts now take the place of God, and the whole course of nature is upset by the monstrous substitution.

"...The way to deeper knowledge of God is through the lonely valleys of soul poverty and abnegation of all things."[1]

The way to peace is to seek God first and wholly. Pursue *Him,* and you will have peace.

In the simplest language, the pursuit of God means the pursuit of Jesus Christ. Look at His life, ponder His truths in your heart: *His* values, *His* desires, *His* goals, *His* love and sacrificial service to people. "Things" can become the chains that bind us. Those who truly desire simplicity must abandon the perceived need to possess what the world tells us we must want. Those who reject the material and embrace the eternal will experience the blessing of possessing all things.

[1] Christian Publications, Camp Hill, PA, 1993

# Life Application: Chapter Six

## Day One:
Read Psalm 5:3. When does the Psalmist speak to God?

What does he do after laying his requests before God?

How do you think your life would change if you spent the first few minutes of each day talking to God?

List some ways in which you could make better use of your time:

What can you do *today* to change things so that you have more time to spend with God?

## Day Two:
Read Psalm 86:11. List some of the things that "divide" our hearts (things that distract us from seeking after God.)

How can a divided heart keep us from fearing (respecting) God?

Read 1 John 5:14-15. When does God hear our prayer?

According to Hebrews 4:16, how should the believer approach God?

**Day Three:**
Read Luke 18:18-23 and paraphrase what happens:

Why do you think Jesus instructed the young man to sell everything?

List some ways that material possessions may affect one's spiritual life:

Take a moment to reflect on your life. Specifically, think about what you own. Use the space below to list the things you possess in excess. (Example: shoes. We can only wear one pair at a time, yet most of us have several pairs.) Please take your time and be thorough:

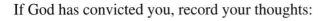

If God has convicted you, record your thoughts:

**Day Four:**
Read Romans 15:13 and explain how trusting in God brings peace to the heart of the believer.

Read Proverbs 30:8-9 and record what the verse means to you. Discuss your insights with your group.

**Day Five:**
Read Job 36:7-12. According to these verses, how can you insure peace and prosperity in your life?

What are some things you will do this week to simplify your life?

Which of the things you listed, will you do today?

What is the most significant truth that God revealed to you this week?

# Chapter 7

# A Balanced View of "Self"

*This is the fate of those who trust in themselves, and of their followers who approve their sayings. Like sheep they are destined for the grave, and death will feed on them. The upright will rule over them in the morning; their forms will decay in the grave, far from their princely mansions."* **Psalm 49:13-14 (NIV)**

*The Christian, like a chalice without a base, cannot stand on his own, nor hold what he has received any longer than God holds him in His strong hands.*
*– William Gurnall*

The covers of women's magazines boldly announce articles encouraging readers to focus on self. Articles with titles like *"How to Get What You Want,"* and *"Don't Get Mad, Get Even!"* are juxtaposed with titillating testimonials like *"An Affair Could Save Your Marriage!"* and *"Why I Prefer to Date Married Men."* At the same time, billboards tell us that we *"deserve a break today,"* and suggest that life is short, so we should *"go for the gusto!"* One television commercial tells us to buy the more expensive hair color because we're *"worth it"* and another suggests that it is all right to lie to our children about the juice they're drinking if the lie enables us to get them to do what we want. One large video-rental company ran magazine ads featuring a likeness of Moses holding videos in place of the sacred tablets, and proclaiming: *"The 11th Commandment: Thou Shalt Want!"* Further evidence of the self-esteem movement's influence on our culture was obvious when a song claiming that "to love *yourself* is the greatest gift of all" made Billboard's Top Ten List.

Scripture exhorts us to *"fix our eyes on Jesus"* (Hebrews 12:2), while man urges us to focus on "Self." The concept of "individual divinity" (the idea that each of us is a god unto himself) is a doctrine of the humanist religion and one that permeates the culture in which we live. It seems that everywhere we look, God Most High has been expelled from the pubic domain and the god of Self has taken His place. The godless folly of the self-esteem movement has left America with a legacy of sexual promiscuity, illegitimacy, divorce, and rising crime rates as the children who are taught that they are "gods" grow up believing it.

While self-respect is a healthy thing, the humanist doctrine of self-love is not only the epitome of selfishness, it is antithetical to the biblical mandate to *"consider others more important than yourself"* (Philippians 2:3). Most consequential, when our eyes are focused on *ourselves,* they are not focused upon the Lord Jesus Christ—and that is *precisely* why all false religions push doctrines of self-esteem and self-actualization.

It is impossible for man to love himself as God loves him, and it is impossible for any man to "know himself" as God knows him. God is the Creator, man is His creation. In his flesh, man hoards the desires of a wicked heart (Ecclesiastes 9:3) and often deceives himself into thinking that a certain thing or person, a specific "look" or accomplishment, will bring him contentment.

| | |
|---|---|
| *The heart is deceitful above all things and beyond cure. Who can understand it?* | *The heart is deceitful above all things, and desperately wicked: who can know it?* **(KJV)** |
| **Jeremiah 17:9 NIV)** | |

Only in the God of Heaven is true contentment found, because only the Creator has the infinite wisdom to know what is best for us. That is, to be wholly devoted to seeking Him (1 Chronicles 22:19).

| | |
|---|---|
| *But your hearts must be fully committed to the Lord our God, to live by his decrees and obey his commands, as at this time.* | *Let your heart therefore be perfect with the Lord our God, to walk in his statutes, and to keep his commandments, as at this day.* |
| **1 Kings 8:61 (NIV)** | **(KJV)** |

It is good to love oneself insofar as we should love and respect everyone created by God, and in His image. It is acceptable to feel pleasurable satisfaction in our accomplishments *insofar* as we recognize that God is the Enabler and that no good thing is accomplished apart from Him. But to dwell upon self to the extent that many do always leads to selfish sin. True "actualization" cannot occur apart from our full devotion to Jesus Christ, and an understanding of who we are *in Him*. Such understanding requires total commitment: the complete surrender and submission of our hearts, minds, souls and bodies to the One who created us. Only then can we see the reality of who we are—-*all sinners*, saved only by the grace of God.

## An Accurate View of Self

In the 1980s there was a popular comedienne who made people laugh by making fun of her own appearance. Among other things, she claimed that whenever she went to the beauty parlor, they made her use the emergency entrance! I believe she was popular because most women in America identified with her: she was getting wrinkles, and she didn't look as attractive as she once did. (She claimed she still had an hourglass figure, but time was running out!) When compared to some popular movie stars and models, this comedienne was not beautiful. Like most of us, she was "average." She only *thought* her looks were offensive because she compared herself to other women. Appearance is so important in our culture that she was able to earn a handsome living making fun of what she perceived to be her physical inadequacies.

Every culture has its own idea of beauty. In some places, heavy women are considered very appealing. Waist-length hair, tiny feet, tattoos, noses pierced with bones, and lips stretched to look like saucers are each considered exceptionally beautiful in certain cultures throughout the world. In the Western culture, thin, firm bodies are almost always considered to be desired. Whatever the culture, the only truly accurate view of self is the *biblical* view because that is *God's* view, and God is Truth: *"Man looks at the outward appearance, but the Lord looks at the heart."* (1 Samuel 16:7).

| | |
|---|---|
| *Therefore, if anyone is in Christ, he is a new creation; the old has gone, the new has come!* **2 Corinthians 5:17 (NIV)** | *Therefore if any man be in Christ he is a new creature: old things are passed away; behold, all things are become new.* **(KJV)** |
| *Keep me as the apple of your eye; hide me in the shadow of your wings* **Psalm 17:8 (NIV)** | *Keep me as the apple of the eye, hide me under the shadow of thy wings.* **(NIV)** |

The term "apple of the eye" is one of endearment; it is a phrase a loving father might use to describe a child he sincerely loves. The Heavenly Father loves each of His children *individually* and *wholly,* and He loves each exactly as they are because he created them that way. At our spiritual rebirth, each of us is *a new creation,* regardless of how we look, and in spite of any sin in our past.

| | |
|---|---|
| *For we know, brothers loved by God, that he has chosen you, because our gospel came to you not simply with words, but also with power, with the Holy Spirit and with deep conviction....* **1 Thessalonians 1:4 (NIV)** | *Knowing, brethren beloved, your election of God. For our gospel came not unto you in word only, but also in power, and in the Holy Ghost, and in much assurance;...* **(KJV)** |
| *All this is from God, who reconciled us to himself through Christ and gave us the ministry of reconciliation: that God was reconciling the world to himself in Christ, not counting men's sins against them. And he has committed to us the message of reconciliation. We are therefore Christ's ambassadors, as though God were making his appeal through us. We implore you on Christ's behalf: Be reconciled to God.* **2 Corinthians 5:18-20 (NIV)** | *And all things are of God, who hath reconciled us to himself by Jesus Christ, and hath given to us the ministry of reconciliation; To wit, that God was in Christ, reconciling the world unto himself, not imputing their trespasses unto them; and hath committed unto us the word of reconciliation. Now then we are ambassadors for Christ, as though God did beseech you by us: we pray you in Christ's stead, be ye reconciled to God.* **(KJV)** |

If you love yourself *more* than you love others, you are sinning against God's commandment to love your neighbor as yourself. Similarly, if you desire to be someone else, you are ungrateful to God for all He has given you. If you are discontented because of the way you look, you are sinning in your failure to thank God for making you unique. If you harbor self-hate because of sins you have confessed and repented of, you are sinning in your failure to believe in God's forgiveness. It is impossible to be an effective ambassador for Christ if self-satisfaction *or* self-pity prevents the countenance of the Lord from being seen in you.

## A Balanced View of Self

Somewhere between self-satisfaction and self-pity lies a realistic view of our own physical appearance and performance.

*Your beauty should not come from outward adornment, such as braided hair and the wearing of gold jewelry and fine clothes. Instead, it should be that of your inner self, the unfading beauty of a gentle and quiet spirit, which is of great worth in God's sight.*
**1 Peter 3:4-5 (NIV)**

*But let it be the hidden man of the heart, in that which is not corruptible, even the ornament of a meek and quiet spirit, which is in the sight of God of great price. For after this manner in the old time the holy women also, who trusted in God, adorned themselves, being in subjection unto their own husbands:* **(KJV)**

*But the Lord said to Samuel, "Do not consider his appearance or his height, for I have rejected him. The Lord does not look at the things man looks at. Man looks at the outward appearance, but the Lord looks at the heart."*
**1 Samuel 16:7 (NIV)**

*But the Lord said unto Samuel, Look not on his countenance, or on the height of his stature; because I have refused him: for the Lord seeth not as man seeth; for man looketh on the outward appearance, but the Lord looketh on the heart.* **(KJV)**

When I tell people that I am a Christian, I become (to some degree) an *image* of what a Christian is—especially to unbelievers. That is why I make it a point to dress in a way that I think would be pleasing to God. It is important to me to always appear to others as a respectable representative for Him. For example, I would not attend Sunday worship or Bible study in shorts because *in my opinion*, that would be disrespectful to God. I believe that if Jesus was physically present in church or in the room where His Word is being studied, no one else would enter His house in shorts either. In the sense that God is ever-present (Psalm 139:7-12), I am *not* suggesting women should never wear shorts or casual dress. I *am* suggesting that we give thought to what we wear when we enter His house of worship. It seems logical that those who revere Him would do so not only in the way they *act,* but also in the way they appear to others. When we take the time to present ourselves well—to be clean, neat, and physically fit—because we believe that doing so shows respect for God, we are making a very practical statement to others that He is important to us. Whatever you think about dress, remember: it is the *heart* God looks at.

*I also want women to dress modestly, with decency and propriety, not with braided hair or gold or pearls or expensive clothes, but with good deeds, appropriate for women who profess to worship God.* **1 Tim. 2:9-10 (NIV)**

*In like manner also, that women adorn themselves in modest apparel, with shamefacedness and sobriety; not with broided hair, or gold, or pearls, or costly array; But (which becometh women professing godliness) with good works.* **(KJV)**

"Sometimes," Carla said, "...I literally couldn't bear to look at myself. We have a full-length mirror on the outside of our closet door, and I purposely left the door open, with the mirror against the wall, so I wouldn't have to see myself walking by. I hated myself for being fat! And it wasn't just because I knew I looked sloppy; it was that I *felt* bad, too: I felt bad physically *and* emotionally. I would become winded just playing on the lawn with the kids, and I was tired all the time. I was lazy about the housework because I didn't have any energy, and then I'd become depressed because everything was such a mess! I knew the over-eating showed a lack of discipline and I hated myself for losing control. My dad is a career military-man, and he was always stressing the importance of self-control.

"I lied to myself for a long time. When my husband and I would fight, I'd blame him for my overeating: I'd tell myself it was stress-related; it was his fault. If something was wrong – and I could always find that something was – I'd blame my eating on worry. I'd rationalize it away by telling myself that "eating a little something" would make me feel better. When I got so heavy that nothing in my closet fit me – including my maternity clothes – I started defending my weight by telling anyone who showed concern about it that "This is the way God made me!" Then one day reality hit me and I thought, 'Wait a second! If God had made me two hundred and sixteen pounds, Mom would be dead!'

"It sounds so funny now – and I have to admit that I smiled at the time, too – but I *really* had that thought! I had actually done such a good job of lying to myself, that I think God *gave* me that picture of myself as a two hundred and sixteen pound baby in order to shock me back to reality!

"I sat down on the bed and cried that day. I cried because on my return trip to the real world, God took me down the road of hard truth. Not only had I become unattractive to my husband, I had become unattractive to myself. I remember thinking: *I hate myself! I have no self-discipline...no self-respect! I'm embarrassed to go out of my own house!*

"I decided that day that I wanted to make some changes in my life and thankfully, God gave me the wisdom to know that I could *not* do it on my own. For the first time, I recognized my over-eating for what it was— *sin*—and confessed it to God. Over-eating is a sin of self-indulgence. It's a sin of gluttony. Excesses in food or alcohol or shopping or *anything* are evidence of the *absence* of self-control. I felt restless all the time because I began every day knowing that I would be fighting against the food that controlled my life.

"I'm still overweight, but I've lost forty-six pounds. It's going to take a lot of time. I put the weight on slowly and I have to take it off the same way. I've eaten too much, too often, for too long. I'm going to win this battle, though. I've got myself on an *eating plan*. I don't diet; I *plan*. Each day I pray for a life controlled by the Holy Spirit. I ask God to take away my craving for foods that aren't healthy, and I try not to eat unless I'm really hungry. When I feel hungry, I drink a glass of water and wait fifteen minutes. If I'm still hungry, I'll eat something healthy—raw carrots or celery. I eat just enough to take away the hunger pangs and then I quit. And I don't beat myself up if I make a mistake. I seldom buy sweets and frozen pizzas any more because I don't want to have that temptation in the house. And when I buy treats for my family, I only buy the ones *I* don't like. I'm past the point where I live to eat. Now, I eat to live."

While Carla was right to be concerned about her excessive weight, part of her discontent stemmed from her feelings of inadequacy because she did not look like the stereotypical American woman portrayed in the media. She was not tall and thin. In the culture in which we live, it is difficult to remain focused on the inner self when we are surrounded by billboards, magazines and commercials telling us that how we look is more important than how we act, and what we own is more important than what we are.

Most of us feel the need to have an abundance of clothing, shoes, and accessories even though we only wear one outfit at any given time. Most of us have two cars, more than one television, and several telephones. In the pursuit of possessions, many of us live above our means. We buy things we cannot afford and we buy more than we need. We may do it because there is a void in our lives, or we may do it simply because we want to impress others with what we have. Either way, when our eyes are focused on things, they are not fixed on Jesus. Scripture warns that we cannot serve two masters (Matthew 6:24). We cannot live with a constant desire for more possessions and have hearts devoted to the acquisition of spiritual treasures at the same time.

Becky admits that she was obsessed with how she looked. "I would never have dreamed of going to one of those discount places for a hair-cut," she said. "By the time I tipped my stylist, I paid eighty-five dollars for a haircut. And I had my nails done every two weeks. That was another hundred dollars a month, with the tip. I never bought drugstore cosmet-ics. I went into the department store and spent seventeen dollars for a tube of lipstick. And *clothes?* That was incredible! I *still* have a couple of outfits hanging in my closet that I paid over a thousand dollars for and I've never even worn them. It's embarrassing to tell you.

"At the time, I didn't think there was anything wrong with spending money like that because we had so much of it. It was not just a case of overspending. But God used a young mother in my Bible study class to show me that it was pure greed.

"Her name was Janet. I scarcely knew her, but I knew they didn't have much because I used to see her family in the church parking lot sometimes on Sunday. She had five children, all under the age of eight. Her husband was a mechanic, I think, because every couple of months they had a different vehicle. Someone told me he bought old junk cars, fixed them up and resold them for extra cash. The children were always clean, but their clothes were worn out and never seemed to fit quite right—always too big or too small.

"Anyway, Janet came to class one morning and during our prayer time, she asked the Lord to give her $19.00 so she could buy a dress on sale at Kmart to wear to her parent's anniversary party. As she asked God for the money, she said, 'I know I could buy the one at the thrift store, Lord, but if it's in your will, I'd really like to have something new this time.'

"Her prayer was so sweet, so humble, that I found myself with tears in my eyes. It was as if God used her words to pierce a hole in my heart. Suddenly I realized how unconcerned about others I had become. All those times I went shopping, I never once thought about people like Janet who have nothing. In all my days as a Christian, I don't remember ever feeling such a strong conviction that I had to change my habits.

"Our Bible study was on a Wednesday. The following Friday, during my prayer time, the Holy Spirit blessed me with an idea. I called Janet and asked if her husband would watch the children for a few hours the next day so we could spend some time together. I told her I had a surprise for her. Excited, she said that would be perfect because she had already planned to go shopping. The Lord had given her the $19.00!

"When I went to pick her up, she was sitting on the step in front of her tiny bungalow, waiting. She was wearing a faded skirt, sneakers with tube socks, and a hooded jacket. Her husband was standing in the window smiling. He had a toddler in each arm, with the three others flanking him on both sides. As Janet literally ran to the car, the three older children began jumping up and down, wildly waving goodbye—as if they knew their mom was off on some great adventure!

"I took her to lunch and then to a nice department store where I bought her a whole new outfit—bra and panties, slip, stockings, and a dress and shoes. I even told her to pick out a pair of earrings to go with the dress. I really cannot remember a day in my life when I felt more blessed. I'll tell you," Becky said, "...there is *nothing* I could ever buy for myself that would give me the kind of pleasure I received just from looking at Janet's face that day! She kept saying, 'Why are you doing this? No one's ever done anything like this for me!'

"I never asked her how she got the $19.00 she had prayed for, but on the way home I said, 'Well, now that you have your new outfit, what are you going to do with the $19.00?' Without hesitation, she smiled and said, 'Give it back to God. It was His to start with.'"

Becky says the Holy Spirit used Janet to convict her of vanity, gluttony, pride, and selfishness. To her credit, Becky *acted* on the truth God revealed to her by confessing her sin, asking forgiveness, and *actively doing something to demonstrate that she wanted to change her life.* "Becky" is one of my best friends, and she gave me permission to use this illustration. Since she first told me the story, I have witnessed profound changes in her life. She serves more and shops less, her family tithes, and she is actively involved in Inner City Ministry. My friend (the one I had never seen without designer clothing, diamonds, and perfectly manicured hands) said good-bye to her manicurist, and traded her silver sports car in for a used pickup truck. She quit getting her nails done when she decided that was a waste of her time and "God's money." Now, she is most happy in faded jeans and a T-shirt when she regularly serves meals to street people. When she is not delivering meals to shut-ins or tutoring kids, she is researching ministries and individual families in our community that need financial assistance. When she finds either, her family gives generously. As a result, God has continued to prosper her husband's business. "The best thing about having money," she says now, "...is being able to give it away!"

*Man* tells us to place emphasis on appearances, but *God* says something altogether different:

**But if we have food and clothing, we will be content with that. People**    **And having food and raiment let us be therewith content. But they**

***who want to get rich fall into temptation and a trap and into many foolish and harmful desires that plunge men into ruin and destruction.***
**1 Timothy 6:8-9 (NIV)**

***that will be rich fall into temptation and a snare, and into many foolish and hurtful lusts, which drown men in destruction and perdition.***
**(KJV)**

*In the flesh,* most of us want more... of everything. That is why it is imperative that we pray *in the Spirit* for God to change our hearts until we desire what *He* wants: Our sanctification.

***I have given them your word and the world has hated them, for they are not of the world any more than I am of the world. My prayer is not that you take them out of the world but that you protect them from the evil one. They are not of the world, even as I am not of it. Sanctify them by the truth; your word is truth. As you sent me into the world, I have sent them into the world. For them I sanctify myself, that they too may be truly sanctified.*** **John 17:14-19 (NIV)**

***I have given them thy word; and the world hath hated them, because they are not of the world, even as I am not of the world. I pray not that thou shouldest take them out of the world, but that thou shouldest keep them from the evil. They are not of the world, even as I am not of the world. Sanctify them through thy truth: thy word is truth. As thou hast sent me into the world, even so have I also sent them into the world. And for their sakes I sanctify myself, that they also might be sanctified through the truth.*** **(KJV)**

To be "sanctified" means "to be made holy" or "set apart" by God; God *Himself* has set us apart *by His own hand.* Imagine that! The One True God of Heaven has lifted you and me up in His holy hands, and gently *set us apart* from all the others.

Sanctification is a *process.* It began the day we accepted Jesus Christ as Savior, and it will continue until our physical bodies die. Until that time, God will use the circumstances in our lives to test and refine us. The process of sanctification comes incrementally as we "work out" our salvation by making right choices using the free will God gave us. When we make a *conscious choice* to desire the treasures of heaven and to reject the trappings of the world, we make a choice to step toward holiness. Likewise, we can choose to nurture the inner self by placing less emphasis on appearances. In order to pursue the sanctified nature of Jesus Christ, we must surrender our self-directed desires to God.

*Therefore, I urge you, brothers, in view of God's mercy, to offer your bodies as living sacrifices, holy and pleasing to God – this is your spiritual act of worship, Do not conform any longer to the pattern of this world, but be transformed by the renewing of your mind. Then you will be able to test and approve what God's will is – his good, pleasing and perfect will."*
**Romans 12:1-2 (NIV)**

*I beseech you therefore, brethern, by the mercies of God, that ye present your bodies a living sacrifice, holy, acceptable unto God, which is your reasonable service. And be not conformed to this world: but be ye transformed by the renewing of your mind, that ye may prove what is that good, and acceptable, and perfect, will of God.* **(KJV)**

God commands us to strive for holiness and He would never command us to do anything that His Holy Spirit cannot enable us to do.

## Balancing Your Time

Recently a friend confided that she was remorseful over the way in which she had spent her time when her children were small. She said she was a perfectionist: her house always had to be perfect, and when she volunteered for service she had to *chair* every committee because she knew that she would do the best job. I asked my friend what compelled her to think she had to be perfect?

After a moment, she said, "Pride, I guess…concern over what others would say and think of me. I thought, 'If I say no, they won't like me.' So I always said *yes*, even when I knew I had too much on my plate already. And after I said yes, I had to prove that I could do the job *better* than it had ever been done! That way I thought people would speak and think well of me.

"I was always edgy because I was always overextended. I had committed to doing so many *big* things that doing the *little* things became a real chore. I'd be helping my son with his homework, but I'd be thinking about the table arrangements for the hospital benefit. My husband would be telling me about a problem at work, and I'd be thinking, *I've got to get those announcements out for the Book Club brunch!* I could never relax because the minute I sat down I'd think of something that *had to be done* right that minute."

I had known my friend only as a mature Christian. What she said surprised me because it was so contrary to all I know about her now. Now she is a walking illustration of *peace:* soft spoken and gentle, sweet, perseverance but patient under pressure, always available and ready to listen.

"What changed you?" I asked.

"After I accepted Christ, it didn't take me long to realize that I was busy for all the wrong reasons. One day when I was particularly frazzled, I stopped to think about everything I was doing and I realized that *not one thing* on my calendar had any eternal consequences—at least none that I could see: Monday, I had book club. The book was a critically acclaimed best seller. They called it 'a sensitive love story,' but it was actually about a woman having an adulterous affair. The next day I had a hair and nail appointment, and then lunch with someone I had *no desire* to have lunch with. After that, I had a meeting at my daughter's school to discuss the purchase of newer and better equipment for the playground, when what they had was perfectly fine. That evening was a meeting at the Art Museum. The *next* day I was scheduled for a fitting for the hospital fashion show, and then lunch with a friend before the PTO meeting.... *The whole week was like that!* I remember thumbing through the pages of my Day Timer...*every week was the same!* And I wondered why I had no *peace* in my life!

"That was the day God convicted me. He gave me eyes to see how absolutely ridiculous my schedule was, and how the ones I loved most were suffering because of it. Before that day, I had never done anything out of a desire to please God. I volunteered because being visible in the community gave me significance. My eagerness to serve had not come from a desire to help others, because—I'm embarrassed to admit this—I seldom thought about others. My motivation was my desire to be accepted, seen, and respected. Everything I did, I did because I got something out of it for myself; I needed to feel necessary and valued.

"God showed me that my value was in *Christ*—not in what I did. But even after that truth was revealed to me, it took a while for me to apply it to my life. For years, I was a 'works oriented' Christian: I knew I was saved through faith, but I didn't fully understand that it was by faith *alone*. Then I saw the verses that changed my life: Ephesians 2:8-9: *For it is by grace you have been saved, through faith—and this not from yourselves, it is the gift of God— not by works, so that no one can boast....* Boy, did *that* convict me! I was *always* boasting!"

She smiled. "It's amazing the way God changes our perspective on things."

I appreciate my friend's giving me permission to tell her story because we learn a valuable lesson from it: The number of activities we are involved in is not important to God. What *is* important to Him are the ways in which we demonstrate His love to others. God is not glorified by one who keeps an immaculate home, cooks great meals, teaches Bible study and volunteers at the Rescue Mission if that same woman is so exhausted that she fails to minister to the needs of her family. Regarding service, there are those who do too much, and those who don't do enough. Somewhere in between rests the one who has found balance and peace.

| | |
|---|---|
| *Better a dry crust with peace and quiet than a house full of feasting, with strife.* **Proverbs 17:1 (NIV)** | *Better is a dry morsel, and quietness therewith, than an house full of sacrifices with strife.* **(KJV)** |

If you feel yourself over-extended, consider and evaluate the ways in which you spend your time. If you are conflicted regarding your commitments, it may be helpful to consider (individually) the different things you do in a typical week, and ask yourself three questions about each: 1) Is it necessary? 2) Does it glorify God? 3) Will it have eternal consequences? If you can't answer *yes* to all three questions, you may want to think about readjusting your priorities.

## Life Application: Chapter Seven

### Day One:

Read John 1:12 and record what the verse says about you:

"I am_____."

Read John 15:15 and record what the verse says about you:

"I am_____."

Read Ephesians 2:10 and record what the verse says about you:

"I am _____."

Read Colossians 1:14 and record what the verse says about you:

"I am_____."

Read Colossians 3:12 and record what the verse says about you:

"I am_____."

Of the truths recorded above, which is the most significant to you today, and why?

### Day Two:

Read 1 Peter 3:3-12 and list the ways in which you can make yourself beautiful in the eyes of God:

Consider your list carefully. Which of these ways seems most difficult for you? Be specific in telling why.

## Day Three:
Read 2 Thessalonians 2: 13. How is one sanctified?

## Day Four
Read the following Scriptures and record what God wants for you:

1 Thessalonians 4:3-7

1 Thessalonians 5:9-10

1 Thessalonians 5:16-18

2 Thessalonians 1:12

List some ways in which "the name of our Lord Jesus may be glorified in you:"

## Day Five:
Read Romans 6:1-6 and answer the following questions: What does it mean to be "baptized into Christ Jesus" and "baptized into his death?"

The Fruit of the Spirit ... Peace                    A Balanced View of "Self"

What does it mean, specifically, when the Scripture says that those baptized into Christ Jesus may "live a new life?"

What part of your "old self" has *not* been crucified with Christ?

What is the most significant truth that God revealed to you about yourself this week?

*Chapter 8*

# Peaceful Relationships

*To the weak I became weak, to win the weak. I have become all things to all men so that by all possible means I might save some.*

**1 Corinthians 9:22 (NIV)**

I smiled at the story of Mrs. Jenkins, who was astonished to learn that her housekeeper was suddenly quitting after many years of faithful service. "But I don't understand!" Mrs. Jenkins exclaimed, horrified. "...Haven't I always treated you just like family?"

"Yes you have," the housekeeper affirmed. "And I'm sick of it!"

Steve Allen was a brilliant comic and a prolific writer of jokes for other comedians. I once heard him say that the indispensable ingredient of good comedy is truth: in order for a joke to be really funny, there must be an element of truth in it that the hearer can relate to. Funny or not, some smile at the housekeeper's words because they have shared her experience: It is not uncommon for us to give less thought to the feelings of those with whom we feel most comfortable. We assume, after all, that family knows us best, so they should be *last* to take offense at short tempers or thoughtless words.

There are always times when we fail to glorify God in our behavior, and often the ones we love most suffer because of it. It's not that we intentionally hurt the ones we love; it's just that they are geographically closest to us, and usually "first on the scene" of behavioral accidents! When Dad has a tough day at the office, he may lash out at his wife because he is not able to express his anger to his boss. And when Mom has a bad day, the kids may find themselves punished for doing something she thought was really funny the day before! Our immediate families are most frequently present when we speak without thinking. They are more likely than others to be on the receiving end of temper tantrums, complaints, and criticism. Unquestionably, few character flaws escape the notice of parents, siblings, spouses, or children.

Someone once defined "family" as a "a group of people in which no two like their eggs cooked the same way." To be sure, it is a constant challenge to maintain peace in one's family, and there is a reason for that. Think about this: God created us as *individuals*, and then ordained us to live together (*peacefully!*) in *groups*. Add to that complicated reality the fact we are each born with a sin nature and free will, and all things considered, God's design seems abstract, to say the least! Though our limited intelligence may deem the idea of *peaceful families* impossible, we may all take heart. God would never have created a plan with no hope for success!

A persistent cause of discontent in the family stems from confusion over gender roles. The responsibilities of husbands and wives were once clearly defined and accepted: Dad was head of the house and provided for the family; Mom stayed home and took care of Dad and the kids. The concept was uncomplicated, and it worked. But all that changed in the 1960s when a tiny contingent of exceptionally vocal women began their assault on traditional families and morality.

In spite of the fact that I was attending college at the height of the Women's Liberation Movement, I never bought into the lie that women are equal to men. My rejection of radical feminist ideas was not due to any profound wisdom on my part. Those who began the movement were so loud and angry that *common sense* told me they had a hidden agenda. That agenda is now evident, as promiscuous sexual behavior, homosexuality, and socialist ideals have invaded the culture.

One of the saddest legacies of the Women's Movement is the discontent many women feel as they enter into marriage seriously conflicted. They are naturally drawn to the role of wife and mother for which God designed them, but cultural conditioning (media, women's studies, etc.) tempts them to think they should want a career and independence too. Consequently, many women marry believing they can "have it all" and do it all well, when very few can. Those who stay in the workforce after having children learn quickly that they have two full time jobs. The guilt they feel over leaving their children in daycare is compounded when they learn that a stranger (and not *they*) heard the baby's first word or saw him take his first steps. (Guilt is often suppressed, but young mothers who finally leave the workplace often admit that guilt over leaving their children was the root cause of much of their daily anxiety and discontent. One mom told me, "I never realized it was *guilt* that was wearing me out because I was too busy and *too tired* to think about it!")

Conversely, women who sacrifice workplace careers in order to devote themselves fully to the family may resent the (perceived) lack of recognition and reward that comes with the job once the novelty wears off. Suddenly they have children and the lack of social freedom that responsibility brings. These former career women watch their husbands, freshly groomed, nicely dressed, and beginning each day with a structured sense of purpose, while *they* stay home cleaning baby food off the walls and making sure the puppy is put out before he ruins the new carpet. Suddenly, all they heard in the classrooms of liberal academia and read in pages of Ms Magazine comes back to assault their judgment: Now, they are *victims*! Such thinking turns one's focus inward, toward *self,* and away from God and others. Fortunately, as Christian women continue to study God's Word they gain the wisdom to understand that their feelings are due more to physical exhaustion than resentment.

Housekeeping and child rearing is no less noble or challenging than working as a doctor or a corporate executive, yet stay-at-home moms are the most under-rated and maligned group of working women in America! If one works at it with all diligence, the career of wife and mother is the most difficult, demanding, and rewarding that any woman will experience. While it's true that we will never be rewarded publicly for *Outstanding Achievement in the Field of Domestic Engineering,* the rewards that come from caring for those we love (and *not* entrusting the job to someone else) will last long after the temporal rewards of the world have vanished.

It is true that housework is an *endless* job. There will always be mealtime dishes and dirty clothes in the hamper. Therefore, it is a job best viewed as a labor of love, an opportunity for godly women to exhibit *sacrificial* love and service to their families as they tend to the tedious details of daily living.

*The Practice of the Presence of God*[1] is a study of Lawrence, a lay-brother who lived with the French Carmelite monks in the late 1600s. Like most wives and mothers, his job was to serve and clean up after everyone else. By the world's standards, Brother Lawrence did nothing of importance. He is remembered all these centuries later, not because he was an exceptional scholar or a learned theologian, but because "he had a mind so like the mind of Christ that he lived abundantly in the presence of God." It is written that Brother Lawrence was found "worshiping more in his *kitchen* than in his cathedral," often reciting prayers aloud as he labored there.

I mention Brother Lawrence because he elevated what most consider an insignificant job into an esteemed position where God was glorified in the smallest of tasks. The sweet simplicity of his awe and love for God and his contentment to simply exist in God's presence is a blessing to all who read about it. As you consider the following portion of Andrew Murray's eulogy of Brother Lawrence, I challenge you to consider the way in which you think *you* will be remembered as you worked in your kitchen:

> "A wholly consecrated man, [Brother Lawrence] lived his life as though he were a singing pilgrim on the march, as happy in serving his fellow monks and brothers from the monastery kitchen as in serving God in the vigil of prayer and penance. He died at eighty years of age, full of love and years and honored by all who knew him, leaving a name which has been 'as precious ointment poured forth'."

Brother Lawrence's job was no different than that of most wives and mothers: he cooked and cleaned, and cleaned and cooked. The thing that distinguished the dear brother from most of us was his *attitude* about the job he was doing. Brother Lawrence was so content being in the presence

---

[1] CBN University Press, Virginia Beach, VA, 1978  pp. 9-10.

of God that the nature of his work never entered his mind. He did not see his job as menial, but viewed it as a daily opportunity to be with God while he cared for others. Instead of grumbling, he praised. Instead of complaining, he gave thanks. Regardless of what he was doing, Brother Lawrence's love and gratitude to God shone around him and beckoned others to enter the realm of peace that he himself occupied by simply finding contentment because he lived in the constant presence of God.

Consider for a moment, the fact that God is present in your kitchen every morning. What does He see? What does He hear? Does He see you smile as you thank and praise Him for your family? Is He blessed by the way you speak to your husband and children? Does it give Him joy to see the way in which you help resolve conflicts? Is your family drawn to you because of the love of Christ *in* you?

"After I read the book on Brother Lawrence," Tracy said, "...I began to take God's presence in my home more seriously. For a while, I even set a place for Jesus at the breakfast table. When the kids asked me what the extra bowl was for, I told them it was to remind me that Jesus was actually here, with us. One morning, my husband was running late for a meeting. He came into the kitchen, threw his briefcase on the counter, and began searching frantically through the pile of papers next to the telephone. Aggravated, he began tossing stuff all over the place, panicked because he couldn't find some information he needed. He raised his voice to no one in particular and said, "I can't find my notepad! Who took my notepad? How many times have I told you kids...'

"Well, Jenna—who was only three at the time—was appalled by her dad's behavior. She gasped in horror and said, 'Daddy, watch yourself!'' and with her eyes wide, she pointed to the extra place setting on the table and said, 'It's where JESUS sits!'

"He was too late to stop and question her, and turned to me for help instead. Now, my husband is *always* losing things because he's so unorganized. It's a constant bone of contention between us because it's a bad habit that he could easily change. I grudgingly began to help him look for the notepad when my son came into the kitchen whining because he was late and couldn't get the knot right on his Cub Scout scarf. I had just bent down to help him with it when I heard Jenna's milk glass hit the floor. In a split second, my husband was loudly articulating his urgent need for the missing notepad, Jenna was crying over spilt milk, and Ryan was griping because I *still* hadn't fixed his knot! In other words, *it was just one of those days.*

"I felt my fuse burning when my gaze fell on the extra bowl on the table and I thought, *Jesus is watching me!* It's amazing how that knowledge changed my reaction to the whole situation. Instead of exploding, I bent to my son and calmly told him to eat his cereal first, and then I would fix his scarf. I handed Jenna some paper towels and said, "It's okay, big girl. You can help Mommy! You wipe up the milk while I help Daddy look for his notepad."

"I never did find that notepad. Dick ended up calling his secretary at home to get the information he needed. But not before I spent almost half an hour searching high and low for it, causing Ryan to miss the school bus that day. But you know what? Everyone left the house happy that day and I was able to keep the peace because I was so aware of the presence of Jesus with us."

In any family it is almost always the wife and mother who sets the tone and establishes the precedent for the way in which family members treat each other. Mom is usually the first one the children see in the morning, and the last one to kiss them good-night. It is Mom who nurtures. From the day a child is born, she cleans, feeds, clothes, cares for, and usually disciplines them because she is there most often. Mom runs things. So when Mom begins the day by yelling and flinging cereal bowls on the kitchen table, she is signaling the rest of the family that things (most likely) will not run smoothly that day. Conversely, when a day begins peacefully it will usually end the same way. It is a challenge to treat our families as we would treat a guest in our homes, but it is a challenge we must take seriously.

## Peace in the Body of Christ

We are not surprised that relationships can be a cause of discontent within the Church because Satan wants the hearts and minds of people, and he works overtime on those who belong to God. The enemy's goal is to demobilize the Body of Christ, and the most effective way for him to do that is from the inside-out: he attacks the heart and mind, hoping that the mouth and body will react in a way that dishonors God and hence, renders the believer's witness ineffective. Whenever there is dissension and bitterness among believers, the enemy wins a battle.

The Church is constantly being scrutinized by the world, and when there is discord within the Body of Christ, others will always be watching to see what we *do* about it. The Apostle Paul adamantly exhorts believers to maintain peace at all times:

*Let the peace of Christ rule in your hearts, since as members of one body you were called to peace. And be thankful.*
**Colossians 3:15 (NIV)**

*And let the peace of God rule in your hearts, to the which also ye are called in one body; and be ye thankful.* **(KJV)**

In context, the word "rule" (Colossians 3:15) means to act as an umpire; to arbitrate or decide. The peace of Christ must rule in our hearts because that's where our emotions and feelings are born. When we have conflicts with others, we first consider what has been done, and then we decide how we feel about it. The way in which we react to any situation is always the result of our feelings and emotions about the situation. In that respect, we are our own arbiters in every situation: we decide how we will react.

Followers of Jesus Christ are obligated ("called") to live in peace with everyone, but particularly with other believers. That does not mean we will or must agree on everything. (As one friend says, we can agree to disagree.) As long as there are individuals, church projects, and doctrinal differences, there will be disagreements among us. However, we are called to imitate Christ in our treatment of others, and to maintain peace in spite of our differences.

Paul tells us to *clothe ourselves with compassion, kindness, humility, gentleness and patience.* Over all those virtues, he says, *put on love* (Colossians 3:12). In other words, "wear your love on the outside...so it is evident to all; so that others see it *first.*" We are to *bear with each other,* Paul says, and *forgive whatever grievances we have against one* *another...*we are called to *forgive as the Lord forgave* us (Colossians. 3:13). God forgave us *instantly and unconditionally* and when you and I sin against Him, He promises to *remember our sins no more*. When others sin against *us,* how can we do less for them than what Christ did for us?

When Kathy's husband was promoted, the couple moved over a thousand miles away. They quickly joined a church, looking forward to making new friends. "The first Sunday," Kathy said, "...I responded to an announcement in the church bulletin and volunteered help with the Women's Retreat. I had been very active in the Women's Ministry in Florida, and had actually chaired the last retreat committee. I thought it would be a great way to meet other women.

"I went to the planning meeting, but I immediately felt like an intruder. The women were polite enough, but no one showed much interest in me, and they weren't very receptive to my ideas either. I felt really uncomfortable, but I did my best to fit in and attempted to contribute to the conversation. For the most part, my ideas were politely dismissed. When they started talking about a theme and decorations I thought, *Now I can help! I'm an Interior Designer; this is what I do best....*

"I made a number of suggestions, all of them quite good I thought. I even offered to do the shopping because I could buy everything wholesale. Before anyone could respond, one of the women quickly snapped, 'That might be how they do things in Florida, but we do it differently here!'

"I was really offended. After all, these were Christian women and no one said anything in my defense—they just sat there. They had probably been as surprised by her rudeness as I was. The place was just...silent. I was so embarrassed that I could hardly keep from walking out of the meeting. Before it was over, they had given me a job on her committee! I couldn't imagine working with that woman for the next six months but I didn't know how to get out of it either. For several days I couldn't stop thinking about how rude she had been. I was angry at her for making me feel like a fool, and I resented the rest of them for not doing anything to ease my discomfort. I was miserable!

"All the while, I felt God telling me to let go of it and forgive her, but I didn't want to. I was the outsider; I was the one they should have welcomed. Instead, she had gone out of her way to make me feel unwelcome. So I decided to stay angry. Then I realized how foolish that decision was because the thing about anger is that it doesn't hurt anyone except the person who feels it. She didn't know I was angry; she didn't feel my misery. No one else did; I was only hurting myself!

"Once I quit dwelling on her sin, I recognized my own. I could see clearly that it didn't matter what I wanted, I had to obey; I had to forgive her because that's what Jesus would do. I would give her the benefit of the doubt: maybe she was a new Christian, maybe she wasn't saved at all, maybe she was just having a bad day. Anyway, I confessed my bad attitude to God and told Him that I was deciding to forgive her. Then I asked Him to give me *His* heart to do it.

"When someone hurts us, our emotions take over. I had been deeply humiliated and as much as I wanted to, I couldn't just *will* myself to stop feeling that way. So I kept talking to God about it. During one of those conversations, I felt impressed to invite the woman who had offended me to lunch. I rejected the idea at first because the thought of spending an afternoon with her made me uncomfortable. But several days went by and I was still thinking about it. Then I knew it was the Holy Spirit directing me. So I called her, even though I really didn't want to.

"She sounded surprised by the invitation, but she accepted and we went to lunch. There was definitely supernatural intervention there, because we had a really special time together. We laughed a lot, and I was actually enjoying myself! Eventually, the conversation came around to families, and she began to share her personal life with me. It was so sad that I found myself fighting back tears of compassion for her. The woman who had been so strong and abrasive, suddenly appeared as she really was— not strong at all, and extremely vulnerable. As she slowly unveiled more and more of her heartrending past, I wondered why she was telling me—a stranger—such intimate details. Then suddenly I knew: she was telling me because she thought I would care.

"Later, she confessed that she was frequently under conviction because of the way she treated others, and that the sins of her tongue often had her on her knees before God. She said she was trying hard to change. Then her eyes watered up as she told me how grateful she was that I had asked her to lunch. It makes me sad to remember this, but she actually said, "I don't get second chances. No one around here likes me very much."

"Three hours later I knew she was a godly Christian woman, but she was a woman who had been deeply and repeatedly wounded by others. She also asked me to forgive her for the way she had acted at the meeting, and she told me why she had snapped at me. She always did the table decorations at the church, and it was the *one* thing that people praised her for. She said she thought I wanted to take the job from her, and that's why she had reacted so rudely.

"Jean became one of my best friends," Kathy continued. "We met regularly and every time, she revealed more of herself. It soon became obvious that the rejection she had experienced for most of her life had contributed to the kind of person she had become. As she grew to trust me more, I continually reminded her of her new life in Christ. Soon, we figured out together that her fear of more rejection had been compelling her to reject others. She had developed an, *I'll hurt them before they hurt me* attitude. I remember that day. She said she felt as if someone had yanked a blindfold off her eyes and she could finally see her problem clearly. She determined to change her attitude, and she did; she was a *totally* different person after that.

"The first thing she did was ask me to hold her accountable. She was going to ask the forgiveness of everyone in the church whom she had wronged. And believe me, the list was long! But by the end of the month she had met with each one, apologized and asked their forgiveness.

"I wish I could say that all of them were Christ-like enough to forgive her, but there were some who chose not to. Jean was grieved by that, but I reminded her that she was not responsible for how they reacted; she was only responsible for admitting her sin and asking their forgiveness."

Kathy could have walked out of the meeting that day, and she might have been justified in doing so. If she had, it is likely that her feelings of resentment and rejection would have grown, causing even more conflict in the church. Instead, God blessed her obedience by using her to help mend relationships that she did not even know were torn. Actions *do* speak louder than words, and one of the most profound ways to demonstrate God's love is to forgive and submit for the purpose of keeping peace— even when we think we have been treated unfairly.

## At Peace With The Unsaved

The unsaved lack peace (Romans 3:17). Since they cannot know true peace on the inside, we should not be surprised when they do not show it on the outside. Though our relationships with unbelievers can be difficult, we are called to accept them as Christ accepted us when we were still sinners (Romans 15:7). As believers we know that in all the world there is not a *single* righteous man (Ecclesiastes 7:20), so when we find ourselves exasperated with the behavior of others, we must pray for God's grace to remember that.

*Do not be quickly provoked in your spirit, for anger resides in the lap of fools.*     **Ecclesiastes 7:9 (NIV)**

*Be not hasty in thy spirit to be angry: for anger resteth in the bosom of fools.*          **(KJV)**

*And we urge you, brothers, warn those who are idle, encourage the timid, help the weak, be patient with everyone. Make sure that nobody pays back wrong for wrong, but always try to be kind to each other and to everyone else.*     **1 Thessalonians 5:14-15 (NIV)**

*Now we exhort you, brethren, warn them that are unruly, comfort the feebleminded, support the weak, be patient toward all men. See that none render evil for evil unto any man; but ever follow that which is good, both among yourselves, and to all men.*          **(KJV)**

Prayer is salve for a wounded relationship because when we keep the situation before God, we are doing all that we can to heal it. Once we have asked forgiveness (even though we may not be at fault), we have no recourse *but* prayer. Our prayers for others enable us to keep this truth in mind: *God is the changer of hearts.* Knowing that God's will is for us to live in peace with all people, we must continue to pray, no matter how long it takes. When someone says something unpleasant to us, we can respond by saying, "It hurts me that you feel that way because I love you. I will continue to pray that God will change your heart." We must demonstrate the love of Christ, regardless of how uncomfortable we feel.

Many times, unbelievers have told me that they have benefited from knowing that someone prays for them. It is difficult to imagine anyone who would not feel blessed knowing that they are thought of and prayed for—even though they may not admit to feeling that way. God doesn't just change the hearts of the difficult people in our lives, He changes *our* hearts toward them. If there is a difficult person in your life today, submit that relationship to God, and His Holy Spirit will allow you to love that person with *His* love. Remember: when we obey, the feelings will follow.

## Life Application: Chapter Eight

### Day One:
Read the following verses and record what they say about your relationships with others:

Matthew 5:43-48

Psalm 27:10-14. Why is it important to know God's law *because* of your oppressors?

Ephesians 4:29-32. After you have meditated on these verses, think of someone with whom you have a conflict. In the space below, write something to that person that you think would "build him (or her) up" and "benefit" him/her:

Ephesians 5:21-24. Why do you think God commands us to set aside our own desires and submit to others?

What is God's will for you when you and your husband disagree?

## Day Two:
In a few words, describe the mood at your dinner table last night:


If Jesus had been a guest at your dinner table, what would you have done differently?

## Day Three:
Study Proverbs 12:18-20.

Think of a time in which you used words that may have "pierced" someone with your tongue. Record the incident briefly:


If you could re-live that moment, how would you change your words so they would "bring healing" instead?


Read Proverbs 18:6-8. What do these verses say about the power of the tongue?



## Day Four:
Read Colossians 3:12-14. What do you think it means, to "clothe yourself" with compassion, kindness, humility, gentleness and patience?

What does it mean, to "forgive as the Lord forgave you"?

Why is love the greatest of all virtues?

## Day Five:
In the space below, write the name of someone with whom you desire an improved relationship:

Why do you think peace is lacking in your relationship with this person?

Read Romans 15:5-7. According to v. 5, how does God equip the believer to deal with difficult relationships?

Regarding difficult relationships, what instruction does God give in v. 7?

What is the result of "accepting one another as Christ accepted you?" v. 7.

What do you plan to do *today* in an attempt to establish peace between yourself and the person whose name you recorded above?

# Chapter 9

# At Peace in our Culture

*You must not do as they do in Egypt, where you used to live, and you must not do as they do in the land of Canaan, where I am bringing you. Do not follow their practices.*

**Leviticus 18:3 (NIV)**

We cannot consider the subject of peace without considering the atmosphere in which we live. Given the crime and violence, sexual sin and all kinds of immorality in our culture, some think it unrealistic to believe that abiding peace can ever be felt, let alone permanently attained. To be sure, without the power of God's Holy Spirit, such peace would *not* be possible. But with His Spirit, abiding peace is more than possible; it is *promised* by God.

| | |
|---|---|
| *You will keep in perfect peace him whose mind is steadfast, because he trusts in you.* **Isaiah 26:3 (NIV)** | *Thou wilt keep him in perfect peace, whose mind is stayed on thee: because he trusteth in thee.* **(KJV)** |
| *Peace I leave with you; my peace I give you. I do not give to you as the world gives. Do not let your hearts be troubled and do not be afraid.* **John 14:27 (NIV)** | *Peace I leave with you, my peace I give unto you: not as the world giveth, give I unto you. Let not your heart be troubled, neither let it be afraid.* **(KJV)** |

Many Christians live lives full of anxiety and fear, in spite of God's promise of "perfect peace." We allow our hearts to be burdened, in spite of His admonition not to. There is sin all around us, and until Christ returns, it will remain so. But *nothing happens apart from God's will to allow it,* and there is no cultural problem that God cannot fix.

As the issue of contentment relates to culture, many Christians lack peace because they fail to trust in God's sovereign control over every situation. A perfect example is found in the radical environmental movement. By implication, those who charge that the planet is being destroyed are really suggesting that the God who created heaven and earth and everything in it is not capable of sustaining what He has made. Those would-be "Saviors of the Earth" attempt to legislate nature by imposing ridiculous restrictions that violate our freedoms. Christians (hopefully) understand the principle of stewardship: we should never be wasteful, nor should we take for granted the blessings of God. But it is foolish and spiritually destructive to assign godhood to planet earth. To do so is to worship what God has created, and that is a sin of idolatry. There will be no constant and abiding peace for those who put their faith in anything but the One True God.

## "You must not do as they do..."

The Old Testament records the trials of the Israelites as they roamed throughout Egypt and Canaan, going from one pagan culture to the next while searching for a homeland. When God finally and mercifully established them in their own nation, He immediately warned them to abandon pagan practices and to behave as people "set apart" from the culture in which they lived. *God wanted His people to be different:*

*You must not do as they do in Egypt, where you used to live, and you must not do as they do in the land of Canaan, where I am bringing you. Do not follow their practices.* **Leviticus 18:3 (NIV)**

*After the doings of the land of Egypt, wherein ye dwelt, shall ye not do: and after the doings of the land of Canaan, whither I bring you, shall ye not do: neither shall ye walk in their ordinances.* **(KJV)**

Regardless of the culture in which one lives, the followers of Christ should be distinguishable from everyone else. Their reaction to the culture and their behavior in it should set them apart from the majority. It should be obvious to all that Christians are committed to live, suffer, and even die, by a distinctly different moral code.

*Therefore come out from them and be separate, says the Lord. Touch no unclean thing, and I will receive you.* **2 Corinthians 6:17 (NIV)**

*Wherefore come out from among them, and be ye separate, saith the Lord, and touch not the unclean thing; and I will receive you,* **(KJV)**

In reality, those who monitor cultural trends note little difference in the behaviors of secular and Christian people. In other words, the followers of Christ have become so ensnared by the popular culture that God's team and Satan's should wear jerseys so the undecided can tell them apart. A significant moral chasm separates Christians from what they claim to believe and what they actually do. Some examples:

> One in five "Christian" women have had an abortion.
>
> There is only a slight difference in illegitimacy rates between Christian and secular women.
>
> Adultery and divorce are almost equally prevalent among Christian and non-Christian couples.
>
> The sins of pornography, addiction, and gambling are as destructive in Christian households as they are to secular ones.

The statistics cited are evidence of the constant and increasing media pressure to conform. At one time the sin of pre-marital sex was unacceptable in our culture, but incrementally, we have come to accept fornication and other related sins (illegitimacy, adultery, homosexuality) because the media constantly provides a platform for public personalities to boast shamelessly about such sins. Primetime television shows (directly aimed at children) feature unwed mothers, homosexuals, and promiscuous singles, all (supposedly) living with abandon, with no visible consequences resulting from their sins. All the while the writers and celebrities, and the sponsors paying to present such trash, arrogantly assume that no one is offended. The result of this wrong thinking has been the subtle acceptance of, and near-immunity to outrage over, *any* sexual sin. Individuals who reject absolute truth in favor of moral relativism will find themselves forever conflicted and confused, living in a culture where wrong is called right, and right is called wrong. Such confusion cannot possibly generate feelings of peace. *Sexual sin was wrong when God's Law was first given, and it remains wrong today.* God's perfect Law does not change simply because a portion of society wants others to accept their sin.

However decadent the culture, the abiding presence of God's Spirit allows the believer to be *in* the world but not *of* it. We have the power to resist sin because we are promised the mind of Christ (1 Corinthians 2:16). We have the *ability* and the *supernatural power* to make right moral decisions, but we must always *make a choice* to do so.

*No temptation has seized you except what is common to man. And God is faithful; he will not let you be tempted beyond what you can bear. But when you are tempted, he will also provide a way out so that you can stand up under it.*
**1 Corinthians 10:13 (NIV)**

*There hath no temptation taken you but such as is common to man: but God is faithful, who will not suffer you to be tempted above that ye are able; but will with the temptation also make a way to escape, that ye may be able to bear it.*
**(KJV)**

## Think right and act right

*Finally, brothers, whatever is true, whatever is noble, whatever is right, whatever is pure, whatever is lovely, whatever is admirable— if anything is excellent or praiseworthy—think about such things. Whatever you have learned or received or heard from me, or seen in me—put it into practice. And the God of peace will be with you.*
**Philippians 4:8-9 (NIV)**

*Finally, brethren, whatsoever things are true, whatsoever things are honest, whatsoever things are just, whatsoever things are pure, whatsoever things are lovely, whatsoever things are of good report; if there be any virtue, and if there be any praise, think on these things. Those things, which ye have both learned, and received, and heard, and seen in me, do: and the God of peace shall be with you.*　**(KJV)**

Paul encourages believers to think only of what is "excellent and praise-worthy," suggesting that peace begins in the mind. Certainly it is a challenge to think excellent and praiseworthy thoughts when things repulsive to God are constantly assaulting our senses. But in addition to right thinking, peace comes from a proper reaction to our circumstances: *"Whatever you have learned... put it into practice. And the God of peace will be with you."* We "learn" that Paul reacted to the culture of his day just as Jesus did. He spoke the Truth in love, and with great boldness because he knew he was right. And though his boldness brought him persecution, God gave Paul His *peace*—peace so great that in spite of his torture and imprisonment, Paul said, *"Now I <u>rejoice</u> in what was suffered for you, and I fill up in my flesh what is still lacking in regard to Christ's afflictions, for the sake of his body, which is the church."* (Colossians 1:24, emphasis added). Paul's *peace* was the result of his *action* on behalf of the Kingdom.

## Lack of action leads to lack of peace

Much of the unrest we feel stems from our concern over the culture. If we hate what God hates, we cannot feel peace if we allow sin to continue all around us. Sin exists because the Prince of Darkness rules the earth, and many Christians unwittingly aid Satan's effort to destroy the culture because of their failure to defend righteousness. For example, where were millions of Christians when *one* woman (Madeline Murray O'Hare) succeeded in removing prayer from public schools? Where were they when Roe vs. Wade became law? And where are we now, as godless men and women continue to assault our Christian heritage by legislating immorality on our behalf? Sadly, many followers of Christ refuse to engage in the culture war because doing so is uncomfortable, but those who genuinely desire to live as Christ did must be willing to suffer for what is right:

| | |
|---|---|
| *Blessed are those who are persecuted because of righteousness, for theirs is the kingdom of heaven. Blessed are you when people in-* | *Blessed are they which are persecuted for righteousness' sake: for theirs is the kingdom of heaven. Blessed are ye, when men shall re-* |

*sult you, persecute you and falsely say all kinds of evil against you because of me. Rejoice and be glad, because great is your reward in heaven, for in the same way they persecuted the prophets who were before you.*
**Matthew 5:10-12 (NIV)**

*vile you, and persecute you, and shall say all manner of evil against you falsely, for my sake. Rejoice, and be exceeding glad: for great is your reward in heaven: for so persecuted they the prophets which were before you.*          **(KJV)**

Note that blessing always follows persecution. Conversely, failure to defend righteousness creates a conflict of conscience as the heart tells us to do things God's way, but the flesh refuses to act because of the imagined consequences: *"If I take a stand on premarital sex, people will think I'm judging others...." "If I speak out against the sin of homosexuality, people will say I'm intolerant...." "If I tell the truth, I may be perceived as a troublemaker."*

Confusion is always the result of a conflicted conscience, and peace and confusion cannot co-exist. *When in doubt, always defend what is right.*

*The Lord will fight for you; you need only to be still."*
**Exodus 14:14 (NIV)**

*For the Lord your God is the one who goes with you to fight for you against your enemies to give you victory."* **Deuteronomy 20:4 (NIV)**

*The Lord shall fight for you, and ye shall hold your peace.* **(KJV)**

*For the Lord your God is he that goeth with you, to fight for you against your enemies, to save you.*          **(KJV)**

Standing firm is not easy, but the "solitary warrior" syndrome is a myth because the followers of Christ never stand alone! True believers enter every battle on the side of righteousness, armed with the supernatural power of the Holy Spirit, and supported by an army of Heavenly Host. God promises to fight for us, so there is never a reason for a follower of Christ to enter battle without confidence!

## "I will go before you and will level the mountains..."

At five-foot-one and barely weighing a hundred pounds, Cindy hardly fit the comical nickname that came to identify her: *Rambo*. Cindy thought the comparison others made of her to a violent movie character was more than silly, but the quiet, shy mother of four good-naturedly accepted the title following her victory over the local school board. She had never meant to be a Culture War hero. In fact, her battle began quite by accident:

"I regularly volunteer at the public school. I have four children, so I alternate between their rooms. That way I see each of their teachers once a month. One week I was in Ella's seventh grade class. The class had left the room to go to the gym, so I was alone, waiting for them to come back. I had some time to kill, and just happened to pick up a health book that was lying on the teacher's desk. When I began to flip through it, my jaw dropped! The first thing to catch my attention was a photograph of a young girl blowing up a condom! The book contained several photographs and illustrations that would have been considered *pornographic* when I was in school—and they are *still* pornographic, if you ask me! In addition to offensive pictures and cartoons, the book contained graphic details of sexual exploits that were presented as personal testimonies, supposedly submitted by teens. And I'm not exaggerating, those vignettes read like a script from a porn film. They graphically described every sexual act and perversity I can think of, including bestiality and homosexuality. I could *not* believe what I was reading. It troubled me so much that I stayed after school to speak with Ella's teacher.

"When I expressed my concern over the book, the teacher showed no interest at all. When I persisted, she actually became defensive and accused me of over-reacting. She said the book was the most widely used sex-education text book in the public school system, and that I was the only parent who had ever complained about it. Later I learned that most parents who question policy are told that they 'are the only ones to complain.' It's a tactic they use to discourage confrontation. They want parents to think that if they fight, they'll have to fight alone.

"Remember, I was a novice activist. I politely asked permission to take the book home and show it to my husband. I admitted that maybe she was right; maybe I was over-reacting, so I would get another opinion. But she absolutely refused to let me take the book, saying that it was against school policy to allow the textbooks out of the classroom. Needless to say, I had no doubt then that something was definitely wrong. They don't want parents to see the books because they don't want us to know what they're teaching our children!

"When I told my husband what happened, he called an attorney friend of ours who did some checking. We found that schools have a right to prevent textbooks from going out—supposedly to prevent theft— but taxpayers have a right to review books, and to copy limited amounts of text. The next day I spoke to the principal and politely but firmly told him that I was aware of my rights and that I wanted to review the curriculum, including the teacher's text.

"I spent most of the day reading that disgusting book from cover to cover, and copying the most offensive parts. Then I put together some information packets that included copies of the pictures and text. My husband and I invited some of the parents of Ella's classmates for coffee, and shared our concern with them. There were seven children represented that night, and only one parent thought we were over-reacting to the content of the book. All of the others were *outraged*, and all agreed that the material was completely inappropriate for children. The group decided that something had to be done, so I volunteered to talk to the principal.

"I returned to the school the next day and told the principal what the parents had said, and I presented him with a written request, signed by six families, to remove the text from the health-education curriculum. When he refused, we went to the District Superintendent, and finally, to the entire School Board to make our case. After they dismissed us as 'radical right-wingers,' we went to the local paper with our concerns. As members of our community learned about the fight, many of them became curious and wanted to see the book for themselves. By that time I had purchased my own copy, so I had one available and could prove our case to anyone who wanted to see it. The book in question was written and distributed by a national organization famous for encouraging kids to be sexually active because they make their money from birth control pills and abortions. Well, as more people saw the book, the outrage grew, local churches got involved, and the protest took on a life of its own. There were media interviews, countless meetings, harassing phone calls, and pro-abortion and homosexual groups picketing outside our home. But by the time it was over, the text book was gone and so was the Superintendent!"

Cindy smiles victoriously. "I used to avoid conflict at any cost, so it felt really strange for me to be—in effect—leading a rebellion. But with each confrontation came an indescribable sense of peace because I knew that regardless of the outcome, I was doing the right thing. There is something really therapeutic about righteous anger. That textbook, and the deviant ideology that went with it, was an assault on decency. It incensed me to know that my tax dollars were paying for it! We simply told them what we believe, and then we stood firmly by our convictions. As a Christian, I *had* to take a stand. I never imagined the extent of the victory we would have, but I should not have been surprised because God was with us."

> *I will go before you and will level the mountains; I will break down gates of bronze and cut through bars of iron. I will give you the treasures of darkness, riches stored in secret places, so that you may know that I am the Lord, the God of Israel, who summons you by name.*
> **Isaiah 45:2-3 (NIV)**

> *I will go before thee, and make the crooked places straight: I will break in pieces the gates of brass, and cut in sunder the bars of iron: And I will give thee the treasures of darkness, and hidden riches of secret places, that thou mayest know that I, the Lord, which call thee by thy name, am the God of Israel.* **(KJV)**

Christians constantly bemoan the sin and decadence infecting our culture, but very few actively try to change things. Believers have an obligation to defend God's moral law. We cannot sit passively in the camp of indifference as the soldiers of good and evil rage against each other on the battlefield. The enemy has taken ground from God's people, and we cannot reclaim it unless we take it back! Those who claim to be serious about their devotion to Christ cannot ignore the biblical mandate to be watchmen on the wall (Ezekiel 33:6) and contenders for the faith (Jude 1:3). To do so would be to ignore the whole Word of God. It is always easier to ignore the sin around us, but doing so is a sin of omission.

## "May I have this cake, and eat it too?"

I once heard a pastor say that Christians should not be alarmed by the state of our culture because "pagans do what pagans do." That's right as far as it goes, but it is not only pagans who sin! Much of the decadence we live with exists because *Christians* submit to the world by failing to obey the *whole* Word of God. Absolute Truth never changes, and God's holy nature precludes His Law from being compromised. Consequently, Christians who attempt to have it both ways (speak like a Christian but act as the world does) will *never* have peace.

Scripture refers to homosexuality as perverse, and detestable to God (Romans 1:27 and Leviticus 18:22), but some who claim the name of Christ insist that our culture accept same-sex couples, thus encouraging homosexuals to continue sinning. God tells us that *all* sexual sin is wrong (1 Corinthians 6:13), but culturally, we have come to accept fornication, adultery, and illegitimacy (which we even subsidize with government dollars). According to Scripture, the shedding of innocent blood is a sin, but there are people who call themselves Christian who boldly defend a woman's "right" to kill a child through abortion. As a culture, we have become so desensitized to the most abhorrent sins, that even those with the best of intentions find themselves confused about right and wrong.

The enormous number of women seeking post-abortion support is indicative of the human heart's response to grievous (but culturally acceptable) sin. When the abortion is over, the irreversible magnitude of the sin is evident. Reality sets in, a mother realizes that she has killed her own child, and no amount of grief or repentance can alter the consequences of the "choice" she made. While much of society has verbally defended her "right" to kill, she alone is left with the consequences. Society does not comfort her, nor does society share her grief. The same is true of the unwed mother who is left to raise a child, and the homosexual dying of AIDS. When he stands before God he will stand alone, solely responsible for the lifestyle he chose to live, and without the comfort of society to defend his choices. Compromise always results in grief because the holiness of God will not allow Him to bless those who negotiate His law. Christ's greatest command was that we first love God, and then *love one another.* Those who truly love, must love enough to call sin what it is. To do any less is to ignore the enormous harm that sin inflicts upon the individuals who form the culture.

*remember this: Whoever turns a sinner from the error of his way will save him from death and cover over a multitude of sins.*

**James 5:20 (NIV)**

*Let him know, that he which converteth the sinner from the error of his way shall save a soul from death, and shall hide a multitude of sins.* **(KJV)**

In addition to the individual Christian's obligation to resist sin, each has an obligation to lead others to the path of righteousness. We can only do this if we are living a righteous life ourselves. We are to be the 'salt of the earth', and Jesus said salt without integrity (saltiness) is worse than worthless—men throw it away and walk on it. A spoiled and decadent culture is the byproduct of moral relativism and a collective tolerance for sin. Jesus loved people, but He never tolerated their sin.

Slightly over a year ago, twenty-eight year old Danielle (then a new Christian) told me she had hoped to be married, but her boyfriend (a non-Christian) couldn't make a commitment. So the two of them decided to live together first, to "...avoid the sin of divorce." Of course the case she made was ridiculous, but she was convinced that fornication was "not a serious sin," and with that determination firmly in her mind, all logic and reality went out the window. You see, while Danielle claimed to have surrendered to Jesus, *she had not surrendered all*. She felt no sorrow over grieving His Spirit by committing sexual sin. Danielle attended church and Bible study regularly, but she refused to abide in Christ when it came to living her life: she refused to live right and trust God for the outcome. Instead, Danielle chose to force a relationship with someone who did not share her beliefs.

"I knew it was wrong when I did it," she says now, "...but I had actually convinced myself that because I was a Christian, God would shield me from the consequences of my sin. Boy, was I wrong!

"I guess when we want something badly enough, we can always find a way to rationalize it. I told myself that God was *merciful*. But later when it all fell apart, my counselor at church told me that what I forgot is that *mercy* is only *part* of God's character; He is a *righteous Judge*, and His holiness requires Him to discipline His children. Even though I was a new Christian, I *knew* what the Bible said about sexual sin; I should have known better."

Her tone changed as she shook her head negatively and rolled her eyes, as if she still could not believe the turn her life had taken. "I can't believe I was so <u>stupid</u>! God's perfect plan for abundant life was plainly written in black and white, but I thought my plan was better. I'm ashamed to admit it, but I refused to take God's Word literally.

"From the day we moved in together, there was not a minute's peace in our house. Brian and I fought about everything. As you can imagine, things got even worse when I told him I was pregnant.

"Once I got over the initial shock of the pregnancy and Brian leaving, I still tried to convince myself that things would work out, and that everyone would be happy for me when I told them a baby was on the way. But the opposite happened. When my friends and family found out that Brian left me, they *pitied* me because I had been such a fool. If that wasn't humiliating enough, Brian married someone else before the baby was even born."

Certainly God has forgiven Danielle's sin, but for the rest of her life she will be forced to deal with its consequences. She says a day seldom passes that she doesn't feel profound grief over the choices she made. As so many others who have been seduced by the immorality of culture, Danielle wanted to have it both ways. She wanted the security of eternal life, but she (at least temporarily) succumbed to the temptation to compromise everything for the sake of temporary gratification.

"It seems so obvious now," she says. "God will never give peace to those who choose to live outside His will."

Polls and cultural indicators consistently reveal that few Christians actually believe everything God says about Himself. Few believe He really means what He says in Scripture, *but He does.* Regardless of the culture in which one lives, *God never changes,* nor does His moral law. He will surely chastise those who defy His law.

*Every good and perfect gift is from above, coming down from the Father of the heavenly lights, who does not change like shifting shadows.* **James 1:17 (NIV)**

*Every good gift and every perfect gift is from above, and cometh down from the Father of lights, with whom is no variableness, neither shadow of turning.* **(KJV)**

*Those whom I love I rebuke and discipline. So be earnest, and repent.* **Revelation 3:19 (NIV)**

*As many as I love, I rebuke and chasten: be zealous therefore, and repent.* **(KJV)**

## Life Application

**Day One:**
List three cultural issues that concern you today:
1.

2.

3.

Read the following verses and record what each says about your personal obligation to society:

Nehemiah 4:14

Ezekiel 33:6-9

**Day Two:**
Read Isaiah 26:3. How does one keep his mind steadfast and trusting God?

How would you define "perfect peace?"

**Day Three:**
Read the following verses and record God's commands to His people:

Exodus 14:13

Deuteronomy 11:18-19

Ezekiel 22:29-31 (Specifically: V.30)

Proverbs 31:8-9

**Day Four:**
Assuming that you are ready to fight the culture war, read the following verses. What does each say about your ability to succeed? And: What promises does God make to those who fight for Him?

Deuteronomy 31:6

Isaiah 45:1-3

Matthew 17:20

2 Corinthians 10:3-4

## Day Five:
Read 1 Peter 4:12-16 carefully. What do these verses tell you about persecution? How should a follower of Jesus Christ react when persecution comes?


What benefit is there in being persecuted for Christ's sake? V.14


Specifically, what do you plan to do to insure that God's influence is felt in your community?

# Chapter 10

# At Peace in the New Millennium

*"I have told you these things, so that in me you may have peace. In this world you will have trouble. But take heart! I have overcome the world."* **John 13:33 (NIV)**

*"One God. One law. One element, and one far off Divine event to which the whole creation moves."*
– **Inscription inside the Capitol Dome, Washington, D.C.**

I once heard a preacher lament that many Christians are so consumed with thoughts of the Second Coming that they fail to see Jesus today. The New Millennium brings with it concerns for all of us: Will there be enough food to feed this "over-populated" world? Will our water be fit to drink? What will the changes in technology be, and how will those changes affect our families? Will we (as most students of prophecy say) lose our national sovereignty and be forced to identify ourselves as global citizens and minions of the New World Order? If the trend toward an acceptance of sin continues, what will our society look like one hundred years from now? Will we accept homosexual "married" couples walking hand-in-hand, pushing baby carriages? Will the traditional family be the exception, rather than the rule in our society? Will our playgrounds virtually be left empty, with passers-by not giving a thought to the millions of babies murdered in their own mother's wombs? What will the fate of the followers of Jesus Christ be, as His Second Coming approaches?

As we ponder each of these anxiety-producing questions, we are wise to consider our absolute inadequacy to control or manipulate the outcomes.

Only the God of the Universe will determine the destiny of men and nations. And while it is prudent and commanded for all believers to take an active role in setting standards of righteousness in our culture, the end result is left to God alone. Whether we are living in wartime or peace, in plenty or in want, in a culture of sin or righteousness, true and abiding peace can only exist through the reign of God's Holy Spirit in our lives. To think that we can experience joy apart from God's producing it in us, is foolishness.

As we consider the various "crises" chronicled daily by the major news networks, we are wise to remember that those who reject conservatism and biblical morality have come to dominate the television and print media. That fact is evidenced by numerous polls confirming that most television and print journalists label themselves "liberal." For example, an Indiana University poll found that only 16% of the journalists questioned considered themselves Republicans.[1] In a separate poll, the Center for Media and Public Affairs found that before the 1992 election, Democratic candidates were favorably reviewed 52% of the time, as opposed to 29% favorable reviews for Republicans.[2] As further evidence of media bias, please read the following:

> *"The question is whether the coverage, as a whole, has become so one-sided that the mainstream press is not giving the public the whole truth. That has clearly happened."* (Sidney Stark, writing in the Boston Globe, March 16, 1992.)

I mention the polls because an understanding of the worldview of those making, writing, and reporting the news is imperative if one is to have an *accurate* view of the state of the culture. By way of example, consider the hysterical accounts of those who claim that famine will consume us if we do not take radical measures *now* to stem population growth. That false premise lays enough foundation to justify (to lawmakers, at least) such liberal policies as condom distribution in public schools, abortion on demand, infanticide (partial-birth abortion), euthanasia, and the forced acceptance of the homosexual lifestyle because homosexuals do not reproduce. At the same time, it is a premise that falsely assumes that the God who created the earth and every living thing on it is not able to sustain all that He created.

The issue of the media's role in shaping the public debate points to that fact that things are seldom as they are reported to be. Those delivering the news always bring a personal bias with them, and that bias is almost always reflected in their reporting. The reality is the major media is dominated by liberal thinkers who (it seems) stay awake nights thinking of ways to create "crises" so the rest of us have plenty to worry about. For example, following are a few of the topics recently featured as lead news on our local television station: *"How safe is that ice you're buying? Tune in at six for our report on contaminants!"* A few days later, one of our news anchors reported ("bulletin" style): *"Rodent droppings in the food at local restaurants? Tune in at ten to see if your favorite restaurant meets health standards!"* Or worse, *"A leading medical journal reports that as many as 56% of Americans suffer from severe depression and don't even know it! Tune in at six to learn if you could be at risk!"* Logical as I am, I questioned how "severe" the depression could be if those "suffering" were not even aware of it!

In my personal pursuit of peace, I have found that one of the most effective ways to achieve it is to turn off the television and radio for a few days and simply observe silence. It is during times of complete silence that God's voice is most distinctively heard. By refusing to indulge ourselves in the (often-senseless) chatter of godless men and women, we gain precious time to spend communing with God. As we set aside newspapers and magazines and pick up the Bible, we gain invaluable insight into the minds of men—insights that will help us to survive in the New Millennium. When we *need* news information, we can choose *not* to watch the major networks. We are blessed to live in a time when technology has given us access to Christian radio networks and news sources, the Internet, and a few cable networks that have demonstrated a desire to report *both* sides of the news.

## September 11, 2001

My telephone rang just as the first news footage of the terrorist attacks on the World Trade Center and the Pentagon appeared on television. The shock and disbelief I felt myself was apparent in my daughter's voice as she asked, "What's going to happen, Mom?"

Thinking only of the most immediate reality, I answered, "Every single person who died in the attack is going to spend eternity someplace." The most important thing for all of us now is to consider our personal relationship with Jesus Christ. Sometimes we don't get a lot of time to decide. II Corinthians 6:2 says, *"Now is the day of Salvation."* As Tracie and I continued to discuss the attack and its implications, I told her how blessed we are as believers to have the assurance of our salvation as we are actually seeing Bible prophecy fulfilled.

Later, watching continuous coverage of the event, commentators labeled the terrorist attack, "more devastating than the assault on Pearl Harbor." President Bush referred to it as the "New War of the Twenty-first Century." On Christian channels, pastors and Bible scholars deliberated the eternal ramifications: Did the attack signal the "beginning of the end?" Was Armageddon just around the corner? Or was the attack a "merciful wake-up call?" Will God give America time to repent before it is totally and irrevocably devastated?

This world, not even the great country of the United States of America can provide the security and peace we seek. Yet that peace can be the sweet fruit of God's Spirit in your life.

*The Lord is my light and my salvation – whom shall I fear? The Lord is the stronghold of my life – of whom shall I be afraid? When evil men advance against me to devour my flesh, when my enemies and my foes attack me, they will stumble and fall. Though an army beseige me, my heart will not fear; though war break out against me, even then will I be confident.*
**Psalm 27:1-3 (NIV)**

*The Lord is my light and my salvation; whom shall I fear? The Lord is the strength of my life; of whom shall I be afraid? When the wicked, even mine enemies and my foes, came upon me to eat up my flesh, they stumbled and fell. Though an host should encamp against me, my heart shall not fear: though war should rise against me, in this will I be confident.* **(KJV)**

I believe the recent terrorist attacks were wake-up calls for all of us. Believers and unbelievers have taken their comforts, their security, and their freedoms for granted. Many of us have neglected our obligation to make the love of Christ known by sharing the gospel. Eternity is only a breath away for each of us. Regardless of whom or what we worship, only One God – the God of the Bible – holds each life and all of eternity in His Hand.

Though many concern themselves daily with what will happen tomorrow, the only thing of real importance is what will happen to each of us for all of eternity. As we enter the New Millennium, the Book of Revelation is *must* reading. It is a warning to the unsaved and an admonition to all believers to live actively, every day, as evangelists and disciples of the Living God. Revelation is a book of hope to all who believe, a book of promises and prophecies—some of which we are privileged to witness as they are currently being fulfilled.

To those who have made Jesus the Lord of their lives, prophecy fulfilled is a demonstration of God's truth and power; it is absolute proof that He exists in the heavens and that He is actively doing as He said, and as He pleases. Whatever happens on the world stage, the Bible gives the children of God the absolute assurance that He is in control. Those who know Scripture from start to finish know that we will face even more adversity as Christ's return grows nearer, but (regardless of how things seem) *Jesus Christ has overcome the world!* And though it appears that God's people are losing battle after battle, in the end all who steadfastly follow Jesus will win the war and share the victory.

While the enemy attempts to torture men and women with thoughts of doom and the imminent destruction of the earth, the Spirit of the Living God is present to remind the believer that *He is our peace.* It is the believer's understanding of God's power to sustain His creation and to bring history to its intended conclusion that will give him the peace to survive the chaos promised during the end-times. The reality of the Holy Spirit's power is seen throughout Scripture, but in order for God's power to be made real to individuals, each must *know God's Word and choose to believe it.*

*For by him all things were created: things in heaven and on earth, visible and invisible, whether thrones or powers or rulers or authorities; all things were created by him and for him. He is before all things, and in him all things hold together.*
**Colossians 1:16-17 (NIV)**

*For by him were all things created, that are in heaven, and that are in earth, visible and invisible, whether they be thrones, or dominions, or principalities, or powers: all things were created by him, and for him: And he is before all things, and by him all things consist.* **(KJV)**

We need not speculate regarding the coming of the Antichrist and the ushering in of a New World Order, because the establishment of a global government under one leader is imminent:

*"The ten horns you saw are ten kings who have not yet received a kingdom, but who for one hour will receive authority as kings along with the beast. They have one purpose and will give their power and authority to the beast."*
**Revelation 17:12-13 (NIV)**

*And the ten horns which thou sawest are ten kings, which have received no kingdom as yet; but receive power as kings one hour with the beast. These have one mind, and shall give their power and strength unto the beast."*
**(KJV)**

*"The king will do as he pleases. He will exalt and magnify himself above every god and will say un-heard-of things against the God of gods. He will be successful until the time of wrath is completed, for what has been determined must take place.* **Daniel 11:36 (NIV)**

*And the king shall do according to his will; and he shall exalt himself, and magnify himself above every God, and shall speak marvelous things against the God of gods, and shall prosper till the indignation be accomplished: for that is determined shall be done.* **(KJV)**

The question is not whether there will be a Tribulation, because God has said that it will come to pass:

*...There will be a time of distress such as has not happened from the beginning of nations until then. But at that time your people—everyone whose name is found written in the book—will be delivered.*
**Daniel 12:1 (NIV)**

*"...and there shall be a time of trouble, such as never was since there was a nation even to that same time: and at that time thy people shall be delivered, every one that shall be found written in the book.* **(KJV)**

*For then there will be great distress, unequaled from the beginning of the world until now—and never to be equaled again. If those days had not been cut short, no one would survive, but for the sake of the elect those days will be shortened.* **Matthew 24:21 (NIV)**

*For then shall be great tribulation, such as was not since the beginning of the world to this time, no, nor ever shall be. And except those days should be shortened, there should no flesh be saved: but for the elect's sake those days shall be shortened.* **(KJV)**

At the creation, God Most High *spoke* the foundations of the earth into existence and by merely *thinking* it, He can lay the foundations flat. All that God created will someday perish, but God will never change, nor will His children ever be absent from His presence.

*In the beginning you laid the foundations of the earth, and the heavens are the work of your hands. They will perish, but you remain; they will all wear out like a garment. Like clothing you will change them and they will be discarded. But you remain the same, and your years will never end. The children of your servants will live in your presence; their descendants will be established before you.*    **Psalm 102:25-28 (NIV)**

*Of old hast thou laid the foundation of the earth: and the heavens are the work of thy hands. They shall perish, but thou shalt endure: yea, all of them shall wax old like a garment; as a vesture shalt thou change them, and they shall be changed: But thou art the same, and thy years shall have no end. The children of thy servants shall continue, and their seed shall be established before thee.*    **(KJV)**

For as long as nations and governments and rulers exist, they exist solely through the sovereign will of God, and by His awesome, inconceivable power. And for as long as God's people inhabit the earth in fleshly bodies, the God of Heaven will preserve and protect them.

*He rules forever by his power, his eyes watch the nations—let not the rebellious rise up against him. Selah Praise our God, O peoples, let the sound of his praise be heard; he has preserved our lives and kept our feet from slipping. For you, O God, tested us; you refined us like silver. You brought us into prison and laid burdens on our backs. You let men ride over our heads; we went through fire and water, but you brought us to a place of abundance.*    **Psalm 66:7-12 (NIV)**

*O bless our God, ye people, and make the voice of his praise to be heard: Which holdeth our soul in life, and suffereth not our feet to be moved. For thou, O God, hast proved us: thou hast tried us, as silver is tried. Thou broughtest us into the net; thou laidst affliction upon our loins. Thou hast caused men to ride over our heads; we went through fire and through water: but thou broughtest us out into a wealthy place.*    **(KJV)**

The question to all mankind is not whether there will be catastrophic natural disasters, famines, deadly diseases and demonic chaos in the days preceding Christ's return, because all of that is happening now. The most profound questions for individuals of the New Millennium are these:

- When the Antichrist appears, will you know Scripture well enough to recognize him?

- When the Tribulation comes, will your name be found written in the Lamb's Book of Life? Will you be counted among God's "elect?"

- What are you doing *now* to evangelize the world in preparation for the Lord's return?

- And finally, when Jesus comes back—*and He will*—what will He find you doing? How will He find you living?

This we know is true: When Jesus Christ comes to establish His Kingdom on earth, the world system will be changed, and knowing that gives me great peace. The Greatest Book Ever Written has the greatest ending ever told: When every battle has been fought, those who stand firmly with Jesus Christ will win the victory; those who persevere will receive the crown of eternal life.

[1] Dale A Berryhill, The Media Hates Conservatives, (La fayette, LA:Hunting House, 1994) p. 13.

[2] Ibid., p.14.

## Life Application: Chapter Ten
### Day One:
The book of Jude, verses 20-21, commands believers to do three specific things as they wait for the Lord's return. List them below:

　　1.
　　2.
　　3.

How does one "build himself up" in most holy faith?


### Day Two:
Read Matthew 24:3-7. The Disciples are asking Jesus about the end times. What warning does Jesus give them? (Vs 4-5)



List some ways in which you believe people are being deceived today:



How can one keep from being deceived? How does one separate truth from lies?



Read Luke 12:35-40. Record what Jesus commands you to do as you prepare for His coming:



Why do you think Jesus has delayed His return?

## Day Three:

In the following verses, Jesus describes the character traits and behavior of those who will be prepared for His return. Read each verse and record the things Christ wants you to do as you wait for Him.

Luke 12:4-9

Luke 12:22-26

Luke 12:32-34

Luke 12:37-38

Now, read over your list and note the areas in which you would like to improve:

## Day Four:

Read 1 Thessalonians 5:1-11 and answer the following questions:

What do you think about those who claim to know the exact time of Christ's return? (v. 1-3)

How do you plan to remain "alert and self-controlled" as you wait for Jesus to return?


In 1 Thessalonians 5:12-24, Paul mentions several things that believers should do and *not* do as we wait for Christ's return. Read the verses carefully and list as many as you find.

(Examples:)

V. 12 *"respect"*


V. 13 *"hold in high regard"*


V. 14


V. 15


V. 16


V. 17


V. 18


V. 19

V. 20

V. 21

V. 22

V. 23

V. 24

Study the list. Where are you strongest?

Where are you weakest?

## Day Five:
Before you read the next question, please record your *very first response(s)*.
Ready? Here goes:
 When you think of Christ's return, what emotions do you feel?

List the reasons you think some Christians fear the return of Christ:

Read Revelation 21:1-4. How do you think the inhabitants of heaven will feel for all of eternity?

When you stand face-to-face with Jesus, what is the first thing you will say to Him?

Being as honest as you can, *at this time in your spiritual life,* what do you think your Lord will say to *you?*

What do you *want* Jesus to say to you?

*He* will stand and shepherd his
flock in the strength of the Lord, in
the majesty of the name of the Lord
his God. And they will live securely,
for then his greatness will reach to
the ends of the earth. And He will
be their peace.

*Micah 5:4–5a*

To contact Lynn Stanley, or for comments on this study
or information regarding other studies in this series,
please contact Focus Publishing:

FOCUS
PUBLISHING
502 Third Street N.W.
Bemidji, MN 56601